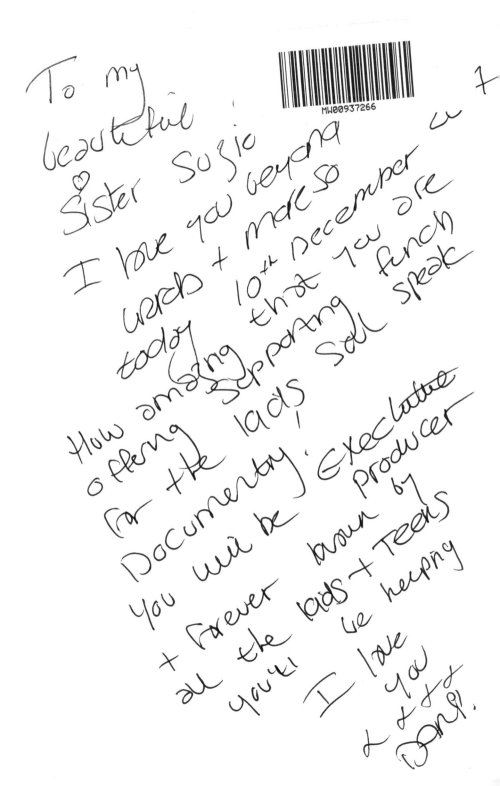

To my beautiful Sister Susie

I love you beyond words + more so today 10th December

How amazing that you are supporting such offering funch for the lads Soul Speak Documentary.

You will be Executive Producer + Forever known by all the lads + Teens you'll be helping

I love you
xxx
x x x
Sonal.

KIDS OF DIVORCE

Danielle Henderson
NLP Prac. C.H. Dip

ISBN: 978-1-4834-6282-0 (sc)
ISBN: 978-1-4834-6281-3 (e)

Library of Congress Control Number: 2016920259

Lulu Publishing Services rev. date: 4/10/2017

Contents

Acknowledgements

First and foremost I acknowledge the great Jack Canfield for his passion and love for kids and teens. This man is a mentor to millions and he was my greatest inspiration to create the Kids Soul Speak Foundation for all kids and teens on our beautiful planet. www.jackcanfield.com

Thank you dear Jack for supporting my first book in the Kids Soul Speak venture with a Facebook campaign. This is more than I ever could have dreamed of. I hopefully look forward to including you in the Kids Soul Speak Movie/Documentary in 2017

I acknowledge my own two funny loving, inspirational wonderful children Olivia and Harrison who have lived through the emotional gauntlet of their parents divorce. I hope Dad and I did a good job.

I acknowledge every single child who has had to go through a life choice that probably was not of their own choosing.

I also want to honor each parent, grandparent and family member that went through this emotional roller coaster and thank you for trying to do the right thing for the children and teens involved. Your actions will leave a lasting imprint on them.

Finally I thank my beloved soul sister and marketing director Lon van Griethuysen of www.lon-art.com for your graphic design talent, creation and dedication to the www.kidssoulspeak.com website and logo and for your unending love and support in this venture.

Kids, teens and adults please email for the questions I can send you to be included in the forthcoming books and movie/documentary. Danielle@kidssoulspeak.com with your great and touching true stories of Kids of Divorce, The African American Kid, Kids of Religion, The Military Kid, Kids with Gifts, What Kids Think of School, Kids who see Magic and other amazing things, and many more books that matter to you

Introduction

It's a known fact that almost half of the kids and teens in the western world are affected on all levels by the divorce and separation of their parents. We can never know the full and long term consequences of the ending of a marriage. One thing is for absolute certain that no matter what either parent may think, most kids and teens don't want their parents to 'break up'. Many hold a secret wish that even if their parents have divorced, that perhaps by some great luck they may indeed reunite. You will see this truth revealed within the short stories that are in this book. You will also read the true and deep thoughts, beliefs and actions each child has taken during this journey.

My aim in delivering this book is that everyone who reads it can see how each kid and teen has come through this journey in their own lives. It will allow you to understand that we can never fully know what goes on inside their minds and that they come up with amazing insights. Some are negative, for example some think, "it's my fault daddy left, it must have been something I did!" I was blown away by how many kids took full responsibility for the divorce of their parents. Some on the other hand realise it is healthier for their parents to not be living under the same roof.

If you're an adult, do you remember how you felt about the adults and authority around you when you were a kid? Do you also remember how frustrating it could be when you had so much you wanted to say but didn't feel you could say anything? You have your own memories and perhaps you still wish deep down that you had had an outlet for your inner thoughts but in your day there was possibly nowhere or no one really to go to who could make an immediate difference.

Kids Soul Speak is the next generation of kids and teens voices. Young people of all ages that deserve a voice and a freedom perhaps denied from adults throughout their own childhoods and growth into adulthood. As you read these true accounts my hope is that you will receive a greater understanding of your own and other kids and that you might also gain an inner healing from connecting and associating with them.

I have chosen to NOT edit their true speech and feelings as they have a true free medium in my books to be 100% who they are and to express what they feel and want to say in their own words. So, I ask you NOT to judge the grammar and words but to allow yourself to read and connect. These young people are our future, our tomorrow and they need to be allowed and equally permitted to speak honestly without barriers or worry of consequence. I deeply love and understand them all and I am sure that you will too.

One of my favourite sayings is "keep it simple" — and that's what I have done in this, the first of many 'Kids Soul Speak' books. I have not padded these interviews with statistics, graphs and global facts that change daily. Instead I have recorded and am offering you the 'soul spoken' words of a variety of kids on our planet, in their own voices, unedited and pure. Are you ready for this?

When I interviewed them, the young people in this book ranged in age from ten to nineteen. They are identified by names they chose in order to maintain their anonymity. Their words come directly from the truth they feel and believe regarding their parents' divorce.

As a spiritual life coach, a clinical hypnotherapist, a long-time counsellor and a parent myself, I am beyond humbled and grateful to bring this information from around the world to you, to children *and* parents who have traversed the experience of divorce. My hope is that you parents will learn something from each story, as those words could be your own child's deep inner thoughts and feelings.

And for each child who reads this book, I want you to know that I hear you, I love you, I feel you and will continue to write for you and listen to you so that your voice can be heard on all the subjects that matter to you.

Thank you for your confidence, innocence and truth.
Danielle Henderson,
San Diego, California
January 2017

CHAPTER ONE

ROSIE, AGE 15, USA

Rosie is originally from England. Her parents divorced while living in the U.S. Her mother, lacking her own visa, had to return with her daughter to England. Seven years later Rosie's father developed cancer and she longed to be back with him to help him in his recovery.

How old were you when your parents told you they were going to divorce?

I was six years old.

How did they tell you or did you know it was going to happen?

I didn't know they were getting divorced as they were separated. We all sat at the table and they both discussed that they were going to separate and they said that my dad was going to live in an apartment. I didn't like it at all. I thought it was devastating and I felt like my whole life had been turned upside down. Dad moved out and we stayed in our house and it became like a maze. You had to be careful on what path you took as it all felt barricaded and so you had to stay on a certain path. I couldn't say "Hey Mom, hey dad let's do something together." I had to wait until I saw them and I really wanted them to get back together. My brother and I agreed that life without my parents together was not a good life. I was six at the time and thought that it was the end of the world.

My dad divorced my mom without telling her, her lawyer told her. She was sad and we left America within two weeks. My mom is European and had no visa to stay.

How did you truly feel about this decision?

I hated it, I thought it was really heart breaking because the two people I loved the most were not going to be together anymore.

How did it affect you personally? What were your deep inner thoughts?

I thought that my whole life was going to change and the common things I loved to do like watching movies with my family or eating dinner with my family weren't going to be happening anymore. I felt like it tore a gaping hole in my life.

How did this affect your home and school life?

I moved schools. I had been in school in America and I had to go to public school in England, which was a big difference to me. There were drastic changes and suddenly I had to wear a horrid uniform with an icky green cardigan and itchy woolly tights to match! We left America and moved to England but arrived with no real destination. We slept on my mom's friend's floor as we had no beds. It was really hard because we had no home and I had nowhere to go when I needed space. It wasn't an experience I think anyone would want to have. Mom tried her hardest to make the best of what we had which was very little.

To get by, Mom sold all her jewellery including a ring she had promised to give me when I was twenty-one; but she couldn't hold onto it. She used the money to buy us winter clothing and to get a car. The kids at my new primary school would make fun of my American accent and they would terrorize me and my brother. Eventually it wasn't so bad as we were highly influenced by everyone around us and soon inhabited the English accent.

I had best friends at that school and one of those friendships ended due to 'Hello Kitty' paper. My friend Bethany was a sweet kind girl and she gave me two pieces of Hello Kitty paper and my other friend wanted one and I didn't want to give it to her as it was too precious to give the little I had to someone else. She thought I was being rude and greedy but I felt like I had given up too much already as I left toys and clothes, my bedroom and everything that had meant anything to me in America including my special wall with glow in the dark stars and my Dora the Explorer bed covers.

Because I wouldn't give the other girl a sheet of the Hello Kitty paper, she and Bethany separated from me and left me by the potato patch as that used to be our place the three of us would hang out together. It was such a horrible feeling and I felt like everyone in my life was coming and leaving all at the same time.

I remember one night when we couldn't sleep in my mom's friend's house because the little room that we used had a beautiful chandelier on the ceiling but the upstairs bath had leaked and was dripping onto the chandelier making it unsafe for us to stay in the room. We didn't have beds at this point or sheets as my mom hadn't sold her jewellery yet. We were sleeping on the floor, my brother and I either side of her on sleeping bags and that six months was the worst time of my life.

Were your friends supportive?

At the age we all were I didn't think my friends truly understood what a divorce meant. To my friend who ended her friendship with me due to the Hello Kitty Paper, her dad died when she was seven so to her nothing was worse than her dad dying. But my new friends didn't really know me. My friends were not supportive as they thought getting a divorce wasn't anything to be sad about. They thought I was making a big deal out of nothing as their parents were mostly together so they didn't know what I was going through.

One time when we were playing rounder's (a bat and ball game similar to baseball) in physical education, the two friends I had left got into a fight and were arguing about whether one was out of the game or not and the way they fought made me feel like I was watching me and my inner thoughts fight. It made me cry and they told me that I was being a baby and fights happen. But I felt they didn't know what I'd already gone through. I know for some people that separation and divorce is a common detail in their life and many kids have divorced parents but I felt like there had been so much going on my life and I wasn't even ten yet.

I usually felt numb about it as I didn't want to let those feelings in. I knew I would be sad. I hated the way my life was and I hated the way I had to live. In my school there was a big hill covered in trees and it was at the back of the school where no one could see. I would often run up that hill as fast as I could and run back down as fast as I could dodging the trees. This one morning it was icy cold and snowing and once again I went to my big hill and started to climb it, as I raced to the top I felt the ice pierce through my pink lace-up shoes and bite my toes. It was fiercely cold and it felt like such a bizarre and intense feeling as I had recently tried to feel nothing and keep the sad feelings away. I got good at being numb so it felt foreign to actually feel something.

Did you keep your connections with all your family members and grandparents?

All my family lived in England so that was the one fantastic bonus of my parents ending their marriage. I finally got to meet everyone in my family and bond with them as I'd only ever seen them for brief times. My dad who is British stayed in America but everyone else was in England. For the first couple of months of moving back, Dad came out to England to visit us but I felt I could count the visits on my fingertips and I knew that he loved me. It was just hard for him to come back. We did Skype and try to stay in touch but it didn't always work out due to the time differences.

How did this affect you?

At school I didn't make a lot of friends as I felt that they would leave me, too. I didn't do great in school and I went through a phase when eight years old where I was pulling out my hair and I hated myself and I ended up going to counselling. I forgot how it felt to be happy. I also had large bald patches under my hair that were pure stress and this went on until I was around twelve. I would get so frustrated and angry that my dad would come to visit every few months but only for a few days and so I went through a dry spell and ignored him for three months. I cut off all communication and refused to answer respond or text him back. To be honest I felt betrayed and I felt so lost because I felt when I spoke to him it just reminded me that I didn't get to be with him. My mom tried her best to get me to talk to my dad as she knew it wasn't good for me to feel this way.

She was really strong during that period of time as she, too, felt sad and betrayed about the divorce. Although we were down, Mom always managed to keep a smile on her face and always found a way to cheer me and my brother up. She used many different ways and one of my favourites was laughing therapy where she would do many funny faces that always cracked us up. I would try to copy her but failed and that just made it funnier. We travelled to school through the country lanes and would also visit my grandparents who lived a bit away. During that time Mom would always tell me her stories that she had written about a big blue and gold dragon and fairyland and a magic flower garden and she did all the voices and that took my mind off being sad. Laughter always helped take pain away.

Did your Mom or Dad meet anyone else after the divorce? If so, how did it affect you?

Dad met an American woman. At first I thought she was taking away my dad. I didn't like the thought of there being another love of his life as I thought mom would always fill that spot. But eventually I got over that as she was really lovely and she knew the position I was in. They eventually got married, but they didn't tell us until the night before their wedding. I was the ring bearer and my brother told a poem about a plum. I was nine- years-old and I was fine about the wedding and thought it was really nice that he had found someone else. But I soon began to feel mad with him again. Even though the wedding was lovely and I met and fell in love with all my new family, I still felt like I was in shock. I felt I had no time to prepare for another permanent woman in my family. I got mad at Dad as I felt like he had cheated in on life in a way as he got two great things in his life in my mom and his new wife and the only life that I had had was ended. It didn't seem fair so I didn't speak to him again, and cut off all communication for another three months.

He thought my Mom was keeping me from calling or Skyping with him, but she really tried to get me to connect to him as she felt it was important as I only get one dad. Soon after that I came to grips with it and rekindled our relationship again as I knew that we both needed it.

My mom met a great guy when I was eight and my brother was seven. His name was Liam. He was really kind and generous and helped me and my brother with anything and everything we needed or asked for. Because my dad wasn't fully in the picture I looked up to Liam as a fatherly figure and tried to grow up to be like him. I moved schools again and went to live in London with my mom and Liam who we all loved.

Although I thought he was perfect he had two children that did not like me or my brother. They were twelve and sixteen, so a few years older than us. They despised me and thought I was taking away their dad when in reality I felt like I was trying to find a new one. They would be rude and ignore us. They made me feel bad and feel like I was just in the way.

I tried really hard to get on their good side. I wanted nothing more than to be friends and to talk to them. They separated me from everything and made me feel that I had to be holed up in my room and could not come out until they had gone. They came over with their friends and would take me off whatever I was doing and I'd have to go to my room. Liam saw what was going on but didn't do much and that hurt. I understand as I was not his "real" child, but I felt that I was and it made me really sad. I changed schools again and at twelve went to the same school as Liam's daughter. She would ignore me for the most part and I used to stay in my area as I got nervous if I had to walk past her. This was very stressful;

she didn't seem to like it when she saw me at school and she would laugh and snigger with her friends if I had to walk past her.

I think she felt I'd already taken her dad and that now I was in her school, I think that's why she was so cruel. I would dread going to school and it was worse because she had promised she would look after me at that school and, if anything, she made my school experience worse. My hair started falling out again and I started pulling it out, my stress levels were very high and again, I needed counselling. That didn't help as I felt I was in an alien situation. I had counselling with different people for quite a while and I found one I liked who was lovely to me. She understood my position; her name was Miss Lilley.

Liam and Mom broke up after four years as there was no romance between them and he wasn't able to show her his feelings. I could see my mom was sad with Liam as she's a very loving, affectionate person but Liam would never hug her. One day I asked her what she was doing with him as there was no romance and I told her I thought her relationship was dead. She burst into big tears, which was shocking and she thanked me for saying that. She had wanted to leave him for a long time but couldn't bear the thought of us being hurt again.

In the beginning it was horrible as I felt I'd lost another dad and I'd have to start again. We were all sad and I wanted them to get back together but I knew it wouldn't work out. We moved again to a house on the river, but I stayed at the same school. It was a happy time and I could finally have my own room and walk around freely without getting in anyone's way or being ignored by Liam's daughter

Do you feel it was the right choice for your parents to divorce?

Ultimately it was the right thing to do. They would not have been happy had they stayed together. Even though I lost something great, I also gained something great. I gained a happy mom, a brand new and absolutely wonderful stepmom and a happy life.

What is your relationship with your mother like?

We have a really tight bond, we know each other really well and we deeply love each other. She is always there for me and she knows how to help me. She always knows the right thing to say. My mom is ferociously stubborn in the best kind of way. We have funny arguments and our tight bond allows us to make fun of each other. She is the best kind of role model as she is independent, free and she teaches me to love everyone and hate no one. She taught me to have tight morals and follow them and she teaches me many life lessons and is the best and most perfect mom anyone could ask for.

She can be really embarrassing at times as she is very upfront and will not keep her thoughts to herself. She does a crazy walk in the mall to make me and my brother laugh and everything she does is her own way and no matter what she wants to do she will find a way, however hard or however long it takes her, she always gets there. My mom is a strong believer in expression and always lets me voice my thoughts no matter how intense they may be. I remember a time when we were out for a run in the rain and I felt like I was going to combust and my insides wanted to come screaming out and I wanted to shout and swear and get my rage out, sadness and pain.

I was so angry at my dad that day I could never understand why he didn't come to England. All his family were there, his children were there. I just couldn't make any sense of it. This anger had built in me for a long time as I was always trying to be positive about everything but that night I had to explode. Mom said I had to let it all out and that she would not edit me or judge me for anything I said or any swear words that might come out. We went into the local meadow and I let rip on my feelings. I let everything come tumbling out and screamed and cried while my mom held and rocked me in the rain and wind. She supported me physically and mentally while I poured my heart out and I forced out all the hidden feelings in me. I was unwell for a couple of days after that but I felt like the knots in my chest had gone and I could finally breathe.

What is your relationship with your father like?

Back when I was six I really adored my dad and felt I was a real daddy's girl. We watched movies when we could, but he was scarcely home as his schedule would get in the way of family time. When we moved to England I didn't see much of him for the next six years. We Skyped and called at times but I felt like it didn't count as he wasn't there with me. I felt abandoned and during that time I was mad and felt like he wasn't any longer a safe haven but I desperately wanted him to be. After those six years of barely talking, Dad got cancer just as I joined the Girl Guides, I was twelve. I thought that my life was going to change again and I wasn't going to have a father at all. My mom took us out of school and we went to America for three months to be with him while he recovered and we all kept positive that he would and he did. My mom always says that my brother and I saved his life and gave him more purpose as she knew he missed us.

Two years later I moved in with my dad and stepmom and got into the American lifestyle again. I found it funny as I too wanted to live the American dream and have the perfect family. Now, I sometimes still think about the changes and the life that I went through and how difficult some of it was, but my dad was always was there for me in his own little way and tried to keep me happy as he knew it was hard for me and my brother to feel like we didn't know him anymore. Since then he's tried his best to be a great pal parent, to give us the dad we deserve.

If you could change two things, what would they be?

Dad missed birthdays and school plays as well as my choir when I sang at the Albert Hall in London, which I felt was a huge marker in my life. I was sad that my daddy didn't get to see it. He would visit England when he could, but sometimes I felt a big gaping hole. I would make plane tickets cheaper if I could! I would make it possible for him to adapt to the English lifestyle as I so desperately wanted him to live with us again.

Mom moving us from England back to America was pretty hard and I don't think I would have done it if it was up to me. I had to leave all my family that I loved all over again as well as my close-knit friends that I had eventually made and treasured. We moved back within two weeks of mom suggesting it, as my dad was getting through his cancer and he is fine now. But in present day I know it was the right decision and sometimes I still regret it but next to all of the time I know it was the right thing to do. I deeply miss my family in England and miss my little group of friends who were the world to me. I have made lots of new friends in the three schools I've been to in a year and I look forward to being settled soon.

What have you learned about adults from this experience?

Adults make mistakes. They don't always know what they are doing and I think that even if you are an adult that doesn't make you wiser, smarter or more intuitive than any child. Some adults shut down the child, thinking that they don't know what they are talking about, but I think we should be given an equal voice as some children have experienced what only some adults can comprehend. Adults are just as dumb as teenagers.

What have you learned about yourself from this experience?

I like to think that I am strong-willed and that I can deal with the messes in my life and do my best to fix them. I found myself during this hard time and I like it because I think I found who I want to be. Of course I would change stuff if I could, mainly my appearance, weight and mind set as I want to be what our society calls "perfect." But I think I'm more mature than my fellow peers are; they might have gone through a divorce but they might not have experienced quite the depth of what I went through to find happiness. I like my best self; it's my goal to be who I am.

If you could say one thing to your mother about how she handled everything, what would it be?

I would say she was definitely the strongest person out of all three of us. She gave it her all she protected us from the harsh reality and full depth of the pain she gave us everything she could manage and didn't let anything stand in our way and she was just like Will Smith trying to find the pursuit of happiness.

If you could say one thing to your father about how he handled everything, what would it be?

I think that divorcing mom behind her back was way wrong. I hated that we had to leave America just because you didn't want to be with her anymore. I still looked up to you but I hated how I felt like you'd left us and you didn't want us anymore. Deep down I know that you still loved me and I guess I was blinded from seeing that you were trying at times to see us but I was so hurt and you missed all my school plays and achievement ceremonies that I was always proud of. Sometimes we would not talk for weeks or more but when we finally did most of the time it was a Skype and I would have much preferred seeing you in person once a year than Skyping you every day. A girl needs her daddy and his hugs. You were brave, too, and I know you did what you thought was the right thing by me and my brother.

What would you change about the way your parents handled their divorce?

I would ask for them to consult us or to warn us about their unhappiness. I would never stop them divorcing but I feel it would make everyone's life easier if they at least gave us a heads-up on their down spiral of falling out of love. I don't think parents truly consider their children's feelings as I know that if I had a choice I would have kept them together having them be the only family that I know as we lived in America at the time and all my family was in the UK. Ultimately it was for their best interests as they wanted to find happiness again with someone else.

Parents can be very selfish and I really think they truly believe they know exactly what their kids are going through. They do not know that we kids are thinking that it's our fault and that Dad left because of us or we caused their unhappiness, or that we were more of a hassle than it's worth and that we were just in the way. They don't expect us to act this way as they know it's not our fault; but we, having had no experience of grown up love, thought we were the reason they divorced. We thought everything ended with happily ever after.

Do you believe in marriage for yourself in the future?

I don't know I guess it depends on whether it's worth it. If I met a guy and he was all nice and lovey and everything, and he wanted to get married, but I don't want to get married only to have a divorce. I think I do eventually want to get married, but I want to make sure that it will last. I want to know the guy for at least a couple of years as I need to know everything about him and I don't want to be marrying a masked man. I want to make sure I know what I'm getting into; I don't want to marry a coke dealer! I believe in attraction and I believe in puppy love, but I don't know if I believe in true love. One of my dreams is to have a family of my own, but at the same time I don't know if I want my children to go through what I went through. I would not be able to stay with a man if I fell out of love and would not want my children to be put through divorce pain so young.

Ultimately, I think love can be confused with true love, actual love. I might marry someone thinking I'm in love but they might just be hot— ha-ha! My parents are friends and Mom gets on with my stepmom and I am glad to see that a divorce like theirs can end with healthy relationships. I wish this for all kids and hope that adults see that they can have mature relationships with their ex partners as it's so much easier on everyone and saves years of pain.

INSIGHTS

Reading Rosie's chapter brings to light many aspects of a little girl, just six years old who clearly remembers all the major aspects of her parents divorce. She talks about feeling barricaded and that her life felt like a maze and she clung to her little brother! Imagine a child of six having such harrowing confusing feelings. Her parents were obviously not able to hide what occurred with Rosie leaving America and having to relocate to England so quickly after the 'unknown' divorce. She shares how she felt like she was in a maze. What she is saying is that she felt trapped and did not know which way was the right way out or whether she would be able to find a route in her mind and a life that made her feel safe again.

She remembers sleeping on the floor in England, having no sheets or blankets and missing her Dora and Explorer bedding and her wall of shining stars so badly that when she was given the gift of two pieces of 'Hello Kitty' paper she clung to it so tightly. So many kids have a similar story to tell when they move from their homes or countries.

They have to accept so much in all the confusion and, in some way or another, they miss the other parent no matter what the situation. The small detail of the chandelier that dripped water making it unsafe to sleep in the room reveals an interesting truth: all kids hang onto events that may seem nothing to the adults but have a lasting impact on children's memories and the feelings left behind inside of them.

One of the things that made me feel sad while interviewing Rosie was the way she explained how she grew to feel "nothing," nothing at all, so much so that when she ran up the hill at school, she was surprised by the biting cold of the ice through her shoes and realised that she had not felt anything physically or emotionally for some time. Furthermore, as the stress levels heightened in her body and she moved from house to house and school to school so much when her mother found a new partner, that her symptoms of stress exhibited themselves with hair loss! Repressed feelings can often come out in terrible ways, not to mention the psychological damage that can be lifelong in some children. Rosie was lucky her hair grew back; it doesn't always. Imagine how that affects children who suffer with physical ailments throughout life as a direct result of their not being able to cope. There are many reports of skin disorders such as psoriasis and asthma in children who have run the gauntlet of their parents' divorce!

In order to cope with her own deep self, she cut communication of off at least twice during a seven-year period. Rosie knew her dad loved her but she could not handle not seeing him physically. That takes great strength for a child to take a stand like that in order to deal with her inner life. Clearly when this type of behaviour occurs the other parent is often blamed for blocking, using the child as a weapon or being turned against the parent who is not around. In my professional experience with working with adults and children of divorce over many years I know that most parents do not use the child as a weapon. Having said that, there are some parents that absolutely do use the child and seem to receive a dark satisfaction in punishing their former wife or husband. Selfish, thoughtless and cruel behaviours occur in the kind of adults who think of themselves first and foremost and do not think about the impact of their actions and the damage inflicted upon their innocent children.

When her father decided to remarry and told her and her brother the day of the actual wedding, it had a long lasting impact. She was angry with him for quite some time. When a parent remarries, the message to a child means one major thing: It states loudly and clearly that there is no hope of the parents getting back together again. And for Rosie to have been given no knowledge or time to prepare and accept her father's decision made it truly a shock and a major negative marker in her world. To punish him, she cut off communication as a way to cope and let him know of her distaste. She is, however, one of the lucky kids who really loves her step-mother and embraced her and the new family with open arms once she had time to accept the new circumstances.

Some kids, as we know, do not feel the same way and that alone leads to other problems with the child feeling more powerless during childhood. It's hard enough in general for them to deal with the divorce and all the heart ache that brings, but when a new and disliked step-parent comes onto the scene, the child again is powerless and has no means of escape or true expression.

Rosie shared the time she ran in the meadow when out on a run with her mother in the rain. She collapsed to the ground screaming and crying and felt physical knots in her chest releasing. She missed her dad so much and had no way to get the emotions and stresses out, so all the stuffed down emotions came to the fore. She felt she had lost him and everyone else who had meant something to her over and over again. She became destabilised as her mother tried to make a life for her and her brother at times unsuccessfully. She saw her mother as the character played by actor Will Smith in the movie 'The Pursuit of Happyness," a parent trying to get it right and settle everything down to a safe grounded life.

What do you think about the new boyfriend she moved in with and his children who made her feel they did not like her? She was always interrupted in what she was doing in her own home, feeling like she had to hide in her room. When she started the same school as the boyfriend's daughter, her fears of not feeling safe were realised when the daughter broke her promise and made her life at school harder. Again this situation happens over and over with kids feeling more stress in their lives with no hope of making everything work.

Think about the boyfriend's daughter, she may well have thought that Rosie was taking her father away, as he had left her mother and the family home some years earlier. It's never an easy situation blending families when the two main adults try to do this successfully. There are so many unknown quantities and we can never truly know what each child is thinking or coping with, we can only imagine.

Rosie's comment that "adults are as dumb as teenagers" is her true perspective on the thoughtless actions and choices some parents make. She has come through her ordeal with a loving relationship with both parents and now has them in the same country and has free access to both. She is luckier than most. She asks that parents listen to their kids and give them a voice and not assume they know what their children are thinking. She is pleased that her parents get along now. She wishes this for other kids, that is, that she says "stops years of pain".

CHAPTER TWO

RICARDO, AGE 13, ITALY

Ricardo had a hard time leaving his dad after his parents divorce. He was bullied by kids at his new school. He developed anxiety and depression and was eventually diagnosed with ADHD and depressive anxiety disorder. Consequently he was prescribed strong medication.

How old were your parents when they met and where did they meet?

My mom was in her twenties my dad was in his thirties they met on a farm they both worked in.

How old were you when your parents told you they were going to divorce?

I was five years old.

How did they tell you or did you know it was going to happen?

I don't remember if I was told, I didn't know it was going to happen. I didn't actually know what divorce was.

How did you truly feel about this decision?

I hated it, but it made my mom happier than being with my dad. I don't know why they got divorced. I try to forget it, so it doesn't upset me. It happened eight years ago and it still bothers me.

How did it affect you personally? What were your deep inner thoughts?

It was a horrible experience. My mom and I moved two thousand miles away to be near her family, and my dad stayed behind. I wanted them to get back together and I wanted to move back to dad, I really did.

How did this affect your home and school life?

My mom was really upset a lot and this always stressed me out. I started a new school and I got bullied everyday. There was a kid called Jimmy and when, I first when to the school, I tried to be friends with him but he hit me. He would always make fun of me and the way I spoke. I had a different accent and he would just hit me all the time. The school had a parachute that the kids were allowed to mess around with and I was playing with it on my own, trying to lift it up and go under it. It was made of felt. When Jimmy saw me he had his friends with him. They pushed me around and then down on the ground then put the parachute on top of me, wrapping me up in it so I couldn't move.

They dragged me around the huge school field and did things like sitting on me to stop me breathing and jumping on me. I felt like they were trying to kill me. I had just turned six years old and they were seven and eight years old. They didn't stop until the bell rang, and then I finally got free. They all ran to the principal's office when they saw me crying and in a state. They made up a story saying that I had asked them to drag me around and they said that I had told them I was happy. I told the whole correct story, but nothing changed. We were in all the same classes through that school, and Jimmy didn't stop bullying me.

A couple of years later I was at another new school and there was a girl who everyone was terrified of. She told me she'd get me out of that school and she made my life hell. My mom told me not to hit girls and there was no way I could stop her hitting me every day. One time she stabbed me three times in the back really viciously with a sharp pencil. The police came and they said I should leave the school as her family is violent and the bullying wouldn't stop. I liked my new school a lot better, but didn't see why I had to leave? Why didn't the school make the bully leave? Even the teachers were scared of her and her crazy family.

Were your friends supportive during the divorce?

No. I didn't tell them.

Did you keep your connections with all your family members and grandparents?

Yes, I did, and in the divorce I didn't lose any family members.

Do you feel it was the right choice for them to divorce?

I honestly don't know because I knew so little about their relationship. I remember them shouting in the kitchen when I was watching 'Sponge Bob' once. I don't think if they had stayed together they would be happy because they never seemed happy.

Did your parents meet anyone else after the divorce?

My dad met Stephanie when I was six, and they soon got married but only told me a few days before their wedding, which I hated. I didn't like her in the first place and, all of a sudden, they were getting married without giving me a heads up at all, which, to be honest, to me is a bit of a d..k h..d move; you don't do that! I hated the fact of being the stepson of someone I didn't like.

My mom met a guy called Jubba. He was nice and they dated for a couple of years, but broke up. My relationship with him was pretty good, he was friendly and I liked him and he liked me. He had an older son, but when he was around I felt I could never relax. When his friends came over (which was every time he did) I could not watch TV because Jubba watched a lot of TV and so did his son and his friends. Mom met a couple of other short-term boyfriends who were weird. One time we were all watching "Lord of the Rings" with Mom's ex-boyfriend Tony who picked up his guitar and started playing it to my mother and singing to her. It was by far the single most embarrassing and awkward moment of my life because he could NOT sing. The other guy, Mario, I am sure was gay because he had all the box sets from the Queen and Abba shows ever made.

What is your relationship with your Mother like?

She passes a lot of wind! I'm just kidding. It's really good. I live with her and we have a pool, which is great, and we live in a nice neighborhood near good people and I am content here. Mom is someone I can always talk to, and she is funny. We always have a good laugh together. I have a lot of freedom; she's a mildly relaxed parent. Most of the time I am allowed to do what I want like going on my laptop, my phone, iPad or watching TV, swimming in the pool, jumping on the trampoline and going to a gymnastics place most Fridays. Mom drives me there, and it's miles away. I don't hang on the street; she doesn't allow that. She is a good person and takes care of me and pays for everything I have.

What is your relationship with your father like?

It is a good relationship. He is kind of easy to talk to, and most of the time he will sit down and listen to what I have to say.

If you could change two things, what would they be?

I wish in the divorce my dad came with us and supported us more and the second thing I would change would be that my mom would cope better with the divorce, that's it.

What have you learned about adults from this experience?

Adults are like big kids— just with more privileges!

What have you learned about yourself from this experience?

I find it really hard to cope with stressful situations. Especially divorces. My dad was so far away that it was really hard to deal with the bullying, which made me really depressed, so depressed that I am now on medication. If my dad had been there, I would have had more support and would not have got so depressed. My dad had a really bad car accident when I was eleven, and I just could not get to him, which made me feel so desperate. I wanted to support him. I was so scared that he might die, and I wouldn't be there to support him. I started binge eating which got me into a deeper depression. I was scared Dad would die as his accident was really bad and most people don't survive that.

My mom would let me fly back and forth to where my dad lived, and then I spent a lot of time staying with my dad for the next year while he recovered.

If you could say one thing to your mother about how she handled everything, what would it be?

I would say "Well Done" because you have coped so well with this even though you let me fly to see dad a lot you coped pretty well.

If you could say one thing to your father about how he handled everything, what would it be?

I don't know how he handled everything as I never spent anytime with him until his accident. For years I used to imagine that living with Dad would be the best ever thing in the world. When I finally began staying with him (I am glad that he got better really quickly), I soon realized that it was nothing like I had imagined and that was somehow the biggest let down of my life.

What would you change about your parent's situation now if you had a magic wand?

I just really wish they would get on better, and I wish every time they spoke it didn't end up in a fight.

Do you believe in marriage for yourself in the future?

I don't know because I am 13.

What advice would you give to other children to help them get through their parents divorce?

It eventually resolves itself, just very slowly. Make sure you know your parent's boyfriend or girlfriend after the divorce. Have them consult you before getting married or moving in together.

INSIGHTS

Ricardo had a great sense of humor throughout his interview with me. It is clear that he missed his father terribly right from the start and, in his own words, "wanted to get back to him." When he started his new school at age six, he was bullied in horrendous ways and this continued for years. He felt helpless during this time and fantasized what a great life he might have if he lived with his Dad. This is true for many kids who are parted from a parent and something of that fantasy may stay with them, sometimes forever. Ricardo's fantasy however was dispelled as he grew older and was able to spend time with his father during his recovery from his accident.

It is also clear that Ricardo was affected by his own mother's apparent inability to cope at times with the divorce. She clearly made choices with the men she went on to meet that were both confusing and amusing to him. Again we have a kid whose mother meets a guy with an older child who does not connect to him. This situation, too, had a negative affect on Ricardo.

He developed anxiety because of moving away from his dad and being bullied at school and he admits that he went from binge eating to depression to being medicated in an attempt to cope with his feelings. The statistics on kids in this situation are staggering, to say the least.

More children than ever before are on some form of medication to ameliorate depression or eating disorders, mental illness and other ailments caused by enduring stress, bullying, divorce and separation from a young age. Most kids do not know how to express themselves and speak up when big changes happen in their lives. They get lost in the mire of the adults who themselves are coping with adverse change, while the children continue, at times, to feel—and become— lost. Many such children find escape in gaming, social media and other forms of numbing. What they need is to be heard, without fear of consequence for speaking their truth.

Ricardo harbors anger at his dad for bringing in a stepmother without his knowledge; he holds her accountable for not being consulted before they got married. He doesn't like the fact that he is someone's stepson when he does not have a good relationship with her. This is the way some kids express their frustration and a need to blame the divorce on their step-parents.

The fact is, his stepmother came onto the scene several years after his parents' divorce. She might be the loveliest person in the world, but at this point, Ricardo will not give her a chance. This is a common theme for kids because, of course, they have the right to meet a prospective spouse. Please, take in Ricardo's story and if you are contemplating marriage after divorce, give your kids the opportunity to meet your partner and let them be involved.

Then, even if it doesn't develop into a healthy two-way relationship, you've given your kids a fighting chance and a choice. They deserve the respect.

CHAPTER THREE

ZOE, AGE 10, CANADA

Zoe lives with her mother and twin brother. Her father left while her mother was suffering with a brain tumor and going through radiation treatment.

How old were your parents when they met and where did they meet?

They met at high school, but I don't know how old they were.

How old were you when your parents told you they were going to divorce?

I was eight.

How did they tell you or did you know it was going to happen?

I knew because they fought aggressively one night and the next day my dad left.

How did you truly feel about this decision?

I didn't feel anything really. I just thought "wow". I was sad, but I knew they wouldn't fight anymore and I wouldn't have to sit through it.

How did it affect you personally? What were your deep inner thoughts?

What's going to happen next? I didn't know what would happen. My mom was sick with a brain tumor when he left so that was a bit scary.

How did this affect your home and school life?

My dad wasn't around, I missed him at home at times and now I don't really feel anything. When the divorce first happened I didn't know what to think; but now, I don't think about it much. School was the same; it was normal and that's about it.

Were your friends supportive?

My friends wouldn't talk about their parents much in front of me as they didn't want me to feel bad, but I told them it was ok. They were really nice about the divorce and didn't want me to feel sad or anything. They all wanted me to be happy in every single way possible. I also have a friend whose parents are divorced, too, so she knew what it's like. I met her in fourth grade and I was in second grade when they divorced. It was nice to have a friend who knew what was going on.

Did you keep your connections with all your family members and grandparents?

Yes, my dad would take me to see his family and my mom would take me to see her side of the family.

Do you feel it was the right choice for them to divorce?

Maybe it was, but maybe it wasn't. Why did they marry each other if they were just going to get divorced? They would always fight, so maybe it's better they are without each other. I am pretty happy that the fighting stopped.

What is your relationship with your mother like?

It is stronger than with my dad. She is more caring and she provides more, a bigger house and food and a place to sleep. My brother and I have to share one room when we stay with him. I don't like it as it gets too cramped. Mom is much more easy to talk to in how I feel about things. We go shopping and hang out and do fun stuff. I see her as a strong, independent woman who works hard for us and I am proud of that.

What is your relationship with your father like?

It is not as strong as my mom's and he is not easy to talk to and I don't really like spending the night at his house. I am not happy with the way he treated my mom and I am more angry than sad, as that's not the way you are supposed to treat someone. Sometimes I just don't want to go with him, and when I say I don't want to go, he doesn't react the right way. He is aggressive and doesn't sound comforting and when he does that it makes me think "wow", this is why I don't want to go".

Recently I have not really been going with my dad because one day he called me and it wasn't a good call. We argued and I told him the reason I don't want to go is the way he reacts to me not wanting to go and spend time with him and I told him that! I texted him to say I wasn't going to go with him that weekend and when I did he called me and asked why didn't I want to go and that he would take me and my brother to the beach. I said I don't want to go because I just don't want to go. When I told him he said we can do other things that are fun but I said I just don't want to go in general. So, he said "Why don't you want to go"? I told him that I don't like the way he is acting and trying to bribe me. I don't think that is the right way to act.

He wants to teach to me surfing, but I really don't like it. He says that one day I would be a good surfer, but I don't like it. I like other things more than that. It's boring to me. He started surfing at my age (ten) and he told me it took him years and years to figure out how to do it and that I was good at it as I'd figured it out right away when he showed me how to do it before, but I don't care as I don't like surfing at all.

I want to do art projects with him, but he doesn't get around to going to the store to get stuff. He gets good ideas around them but doesn't get the stuff. I want him to act the right way to me when I say I don't want to go and I want him to have better ideas of what to do with me rather than the beach.

Some kids with divorced parents have really good relationships with both parents. I don't have a good relationship with my dad but I have a good one with my mom. Some daughters are supposed to have a really good father -daughter relationship with their dads but I really don't have that.

If you could change two things, what would they be?

My dad would have to be nicer to my mom, and he would need to be better at comforting me and my brother.

What have you learned about Adults from this experience?

I have definitely learned more about who my dad is but not really anything more than that. It is different from the way I saw him when my parents were married. I used to think of my dad as a really nice caring person, but now I notice things that are way different from what I used to think. He always thinks the worst of my mom and, when I don't want to go with him to visit, he acts in the totally wrong way. My mom has always been really sweet, caring and loving.

What have you learned about yourself from this experience?

I have learned that I know how to manoeuvre around problems that occur when my parents have fights. I figure out how to solve them instead of sitting there trying to figure out what's going on. When my dad says something bad about my mom I know automatically that it is not true and that it is just his problem that he is trying to figure out. I realise that when my dad behaves in the wrong way, I stand up for myself and tell him that it is not ok and this is why I don't like going with him.

If you could say one thing to your mother about how she handled everything, what would it be?

"I am proud of the way you handled everything, the way you did everything right, the way you provide for us, our home and roof over our heads and be able to go through it all (radiation and treatment for a brain tumor) and still make sure we were all provided for".

If you could say one thing to your father about how he handled everything, what would it be?

"You are not doing the right thing and jumping to conclusions and thinking the worst of my mom and making it look like she is the bad person, even though you are the one making all the mistakes and doing everything wrong!"

What would you change about your parents' situation now if you had a magic wand?

I would change the way my dad reacts to my mom in anything she says, and for him to stop being bad about how she is the person who is doing everything wrong and how he is doing everything right, even though it is the other way around. At times I would like a better relationship with him, but it can go either way.

Do you believe in marriage for yourself in the future?

Yeah. I'd like a happy future with a nice family and everything. For everything to be normal and for my children not to go through what I had to go through when I was a kid.

What advice would you give to other children to help them get through their parents divorce?

Just say what you need to say and feel free to, if you have something that you really feel you should say you should say it. It won't hurt you or anyone else. All it will do is make everyone feel better. If you feel like you don't like something that is going on, you should tell the person that is doing what you don't like and tell them how you feel about it.

INSIGHTS

Zoe speaks constantly about her dad not doing 'the right thing' in her eyes. Who can blame her for her perspective? She saw first-hand a man leaving a woman with a life threatening illness, her own beloved mother. Her dad, who is of course her first male role model, showed her a behavior that she clearly struggles to come to terms with. What message is he giving his daughter about fathers and men in general who quit when the going gets tough? Whether she is aware or not she is unconsciously and possibly consciously punishing him.

Zoe is frustrated as most 10 years olds would be, that when she suggests activities with her dad, such as art projects he at first engages. He offers ideas about what they could do, but doesn't follow through by getting art supplies. Instead, he appears to assert his desire to teach her how to surf. Is it because this is something he is good at and he wants to pass it onto her? It doesn't matter to Zoe at all as you can read for yourself. She needs her dad to be comforting (her own words) to her and her brother. Is this because he was not a comfort to her own mother and she saw him 'leave' when her mother was at her lowest point of her illness?

I work with many kids navigating the challenges of divorce and Zoe strikes me as a particularly emotionally mature little girl. She's had to grow up faster than most, due to the circumstances surrounding her mother's illness. The most glaringly obvious 'thing' for me is to recognize that she simply does not trust her father at all. She has decided that when he is unkind about her mother that what he is saying is always not true and it's (her own words) his problem. She is fiercely protective of her mother who she see's as loving, caring and sweet and, despite the illness_ she has thankfully overcome—she has not changed towards Zoe during this time. Her mother represents true stability in her life, and she clings to that and feels unsafe when she spends time with her dad.

It is unlikely at this point and, indeed, the near future that Zoe's refusal to allow a healthy father-daughter relationship will change. The wounds inflicted on her during her parents' divorce run deep, and she has not healed her scars. Many kids, for varied reasons, will punish their parents for what they feel was done wrong. Kids are taught to respect adults and not be rude or speak out on subjects deemed 'adult'. From my own perspective, I see this as absolute nonsense and know from experience that it serves no one and can affect a child in ways that can carry through their entire lives.

To resolve Zoe's issues, her dad would do well to take stock of his actions, no matter what reason he had for leaving. If he sat down with her and apologised and did not say unkind things about her mother, perhaps he'd stand a chance of rescuing his relationship with his daughter. What's more important, for a parent to be 'right' in his or her own mind or to be unconditionally loving to their own child and making an effort to ease the pain and suffering inflicted on the child, due to their actions that the child can not grasp or understand? Zoe continually watches for her father to do the right thing as she see's it. Do you think, given her story, that he will?

CHAPTER FOUR

BOB-JOHNSON, AGE 10, CANADA, (twin brother to Zoe).

How old were your parents when they met and where did they meet?

I am not sure about that, they knew each other in school and met years later and married.

How old were you when your parents told you they were going to Divorce?

They didn't really tell me but I was eight going on nine and my mum was sick with a brain tumor, and there was this whole thing with 'soup'. My mom asked my dad to get soup and he forgot and he walked away from her and called her a name, it was the B name! She told him to get back into the kitchen and they fought and she hit him a couple of times. Then my grandmother came in and broke it up, and after that, my mom said my dad had to stay at his mom's for a little while.

How did they tell you or did you know it was going to happen?

After my mom told him to leave for a couple of days, I figured he was not going to come back and that they would split up and get a divorce.

How did you truly feel about this decision?

I am glad I am talking about it now. It feels like a weight off my chest. When they told me I wasn't really sad, I felt uneasy. I wasn't happy about it.

How did it affect you personally? What were your deep inner thoughts?

I thought that my life was going to change a lot with me going between my dad's and mom's and I thought it was going to be rough as I wouldn't always be prepared. Sometimes he (dad) would just show up surprisingly and I wasn't really ready and sometimes I would want to stay with my mom and not go with him, but afterwards I would feel bad for my dad.

How did this affect your home and school life?

It was a lot different around the house. At school it didn't really change at all. My mom was at home and my dad wasn't around the house. He wasn't always around when he lived with us as he went to work. So it wasn't much different. When he would come home from work, he wouldn't be there; he would be at his place as they had split up and he should have been home. So that was the main difference. My twin sister didn't show any emotion for it, I didn't notice her acting any different. On the birthday after he left, my dad wasn't there to light our candles. That felt weird. I feel like my dad should have found a way to stay here, as my mom was sick with her brain tumor and she was getting radiation and it made her very tired. He should have helped her with us, as she still had to do all the driving but sometimes we didn't make it to sports or swimming because she was too tired. I felt bad for her, and she shouldn't have had to do all the driving because she was really sick.

Were your friends supportive?

None of my friends had gone through this stuff and they didn't really know how to help because I wasn't really telling them and I wasn't really sad at school.

Did you keep your connections with all your family members and grandparents?

I stayed in touch with my dad and my mom and I didn't really have my grandma on my dad's side's phone number. For a little while I didn't have a phone. My dad lived at my grandma's house for a little while so I saw her. She was really nice; she's not mean or anything and she's good to me.

How did this affect you?

I still see them all and I would go to family events with my dad and Xmas so I would see the other family members, my uncles, aunts and cousins.

Do you feel it was the right choice for them to divorce?

If they didn't get a divorce, there would have been fights in the household so kind of and kind of not. I don't think they should have gotten a divorce when my mom was sick. I don't want either of them getting hurt, so it's better that they did divorce so the fights stopped. They didn't fight much when they were together, just mostly towards the end. One time right before my dad left, he made dinner and I saw them look at each other for a long time like they hated each other and my mom made my dad sleep on the couch. I didn't have an expression for it. I didn't have a feeling for it I just felt they wouldn't sleep together that night, as they were mad at each other. I slept downstairs with my dad as I was watching TV and I think I fell asleep watching TV and around 1pm in the morning I woke up and he was watching a movie. I don't think he knew I was awake.

What is your relationship with your mother like?

It is pretty strong, but every now and again we will get into a little bit of an argument. Usually I will feel bad. It's normally before school and when I get home I apologise as I feel bad in school if we have had an argument and I don't do well as I can't focus and I keep thinking about it. I like how she supports us whether it's sports or if I'm playing basketball and recently I was playing with my sister and her ex-boyfriend and she was clapping and I liked that. She finds a way to fix our problems. She is funny at times and kind, I like that she is a loving, caring and non-abusive mother. She doesn't like it when my dog makes messes in the house and she says if that dog didn't love me so much and I didn't love that dog, she wouldn't let me keep him.

What is your relationship with your father like?

It is also a really strong relationship. We don't get into arguments very often. He likes to do mountain bike riding, hockey and baseball and he practices with me. He got me a bike, so we can ride together and sometimes on weekends we hang around the house. Sometimes he says not very positive things about my mom and I don't like it. Last year he was saying something about my mom having a boyfriend when she didn't and he said he had seen texts. Eventually I got sick of it and asked him to stop and he did. A long time ago, she would say the odd not very positive thing about him, such as "He should not have left our family". But she doesn't say anything negative about him anymore. They just argue on the phone sometimes, but she doesn't say anything to me about him and I'm glad about that.

If you could change two things, what would they be?

I would make it so they didn't have that big fight, but my mom says the relationship was already unstable. Eventually they would have kept arguing and they would have divorced. I really don't know what caused it to be an unstable relationship. My dad was mean to her before she got sick, and she would be mean to him also.

What have you learned about adults from this experience?

I learned that they are not always right and they don't really understand how I feel sometimes about the divorce. For a little while I felt like I had done something to make them divorce. I felt like I somehow could have stopped it. Maybe I could have, but I am not sure exactly sure.

What have you learned about yourself from this experience?

I have learned that I don't break down or give up and I try to find a way to make the best of things. If you try to find a way to make the best of things, good things will come to you. There is always hope in a bad situation. I don't think it's easy for my mom as she needs to raise us. I am emotionally strong and I am not going to be picked on and I stand up for myself.

If you could say one thing to your mother about how she handled everything, what would it be?

It is really amazing how she managed to do all this and she was so sick and she was a single mother and how she managed to keep us in this house and keep food on the table for us. That is what I would say.

If you could say one thing to your father about how he handled everything, what would it be?

"I think that you should not have called my mom the B word" and that if he had not called her that and done what she asked and went and got the soup for her, then maybe the relationship would have lasted a little longer while she was getting better. He had the power to stop that, and he didn't think of it and he should have.

What would you change about your parent's situation now, if you had a magic wand?

I have been asked that before at a clinic we went to about divorce. It was called 'Kids Turn' and it showed that kids were allowed to speak, but I wasn't really sure what I would do and I'm still not sure, but I do know that if there was one thing I could stop, I would have zipped my dad's mouth closed before he said it.

Do you believe in marriage for yourself in the future?

Yes. Based on what I saw, if I ever get into that situation, I will try to remember that situation and what to say and what not to say. If I do that, maybe I will have a good relationship.

What advice would you give to other children to help them get through their parents divorce?

If they feel like they did something to make it happen, they did not. It was a choice their parents made and, if they feel like they could stop it, they can't. Try to make the best of things. Think about all the good things in life that you have and be happy that you are alive and that at least you still have parents. If you visit both of them at least you still get to see them. It depends what perspective the child has on the divorce, if they see they have a roof over their head and they have mostly what they need then they are lucky. If they are having any suicidal thoughts, think of how many people will miss you and that they have a lot to live for because they are just a kid and they have a long life ahead of them.

INSIGHTS

Bob-Johnson is a very sweet kid, your typical Canadian smiling, hockey-playing, trampoline-jumping, healthy boy. Many kids around the world like him remember the moment their world was impacted forever by the news of their parent's divorce, an event that took place and left a permanent imprint in their mind when they knew life would change forever. You could compare it to the death of Kennedy or Princess Diana and the question adults ask each other "Where were you the day it happened?" Obviously for the kid involved in that 'moment' his or her trauma is far far greater than that of losing any famous or noted person outside of their family. And for Bob-Johnson that life-changing moment was an argument his parents had over "soup".

What pleased me as I interviewed this delightful child was the physical weight that he said felt lifted off his chest. He took huge breaths and tapped his chest, releasing pent-up emotion as he clearly had not truly expressed himself about how he deeply felt, up until this point. He witnessed the final argument between his parents in the kitchen that the grandmother came in to break up. He saw his mother slap his dad in frustration as she felt he'd let her down; she was sick with a brain tumor; she wanted soup; he forgot to get it, and refused to

drive three minutes to get it. This mother had been going through
many months of radiation and chemotherapy.

*I am very close with Zoe and Bob-Johnson's mother and admire the
way she has coped during and after her treatment for a brain tumor.
She has determined that her kids need strong male role models and,
to this end, she has circled them with her own group of strong men so
that her kids can look up to them and feel safe with males. It reminds
me of people like Elisabeth Hurley whose own son has at least six
godparents, including Sir Elton John and the actor Hugh Grant.*

*Of course the marriage didn't end just because of that one situation
(the soup), but all kids need an anchor point to create a story in their
minds as to why their parents marriage broke down so completely.
Note how his first memory after his father left the house was that he
was not there to light birthday candles for him and his twin sister's
birthday.*

*There is a lot of guilt in Bob-Johnson's chapter, as he clearly feels sad
that his mother was sick and alone with all the responsibilities and
he wanted his dad to step up and help the family. When a parent is
sick, most children deep down fear that parent will die. We are hard-
wired in the brain to have these thoughts either as a way to mentally
prepare or to be on high alert that there is a risk to the immediate
family. Fortunately most sick parents recover from illness and normal
life resumes but for a child who is terrified the parent might die. You
can imagine what it must have felt like for these twins to endure
two parents arguing and then have to watch the supposedly strong
healthy one leave. Such the deep-seated trauma scars a child and
could lead to years of anxiety-ridden behaviours.*

*Note how Bob-Johnson feels if he has an argument with his mother
in the morning before school. He carries it inside himself all day; he*

cannot concentrate on anything but getting out of school and seeing his mother to apologise and put everything back in it's rightful place in his heart and mind. Some might say it's normal for a kid to carry sadness from an earlier argument and, of course, he'd want to make it up with his mother. But just think for a moment that some kids may never be able to truly feel their feelings and figure things out in a more common sense way.

Bob-Johnson is very affected by the negative comments his dad makes about his mom and it got so intense for him that he found the courage to ask him to stop. His mother, he claims, does not say negative things to him about his dad only that she thinks he should never have left the family. He also shared that he felt responsible for the divorce, which is always sad to hear from a child as so many convince themselves it's their fault in some way and they could have made the marriage last longer if they had not done this behaviour or that behaviour. But, of course, it is never their fault.

We know that a child should ever be allowed to carry guilt for either parent and, in situations like this one, it's even more important for the healthy parent to double up and take the strain of the other, without punishing them in any way, and allowing the children living in the home to see a supportive parent who can handle the situation in front of them. The way a parent behaves always has a lasting effect on a child! Kids will often carry the misdeeds of a parent as their own penance throughout life because they are unconsciously trying to heal the terrible hurt.

CHAPTER FIVE

ISABELLE, AGE 19, FRANCE

Isabelle is a teenager who has a mother with a mental illness that defined the behaviours between both parents. Her mother was particularly emotionally cruel to Isabelle who suffered many lonely years.

How old were your parents when they met and where did they meet?

I know virtually nothing about the early stages of my parents' relationship. I was just a toddler when they divorced and the divorce itself was not amicable and so I never had the opportunity to find out any details of how and when they met. Sadly, I've never felt comfortable broaching the subject with either of them, nor do I think they'd be particularly receptive to the probing.

How old were you when your parents told you they were going to divorce?

I think I was around three years old.

How did they tell you or did you know it was going to happen?

I have only two memories from around the time my parents divorced. I remember being in the living room while my parents were arguing over who would be taking the car that day. My mom needed it to take me to school and my dad needed it to go to work. And then I remember my mom asking me one evening if I understood why they had decided to separate and I said that it was because they both wanted the car. I don't remember what my mom said to me in response or how much time had elapsed between the two incidents or whether they're even real memories!

How did you truly feel about this decision?

Being so young, I didn't truly understand what was happening, or even understand the concept of marriage and divorce. The hardest part was the animosity between my parents following their separation and the constant conflict that I was dragged into the middle of.

How did it affect you personally, what were your deep inner thoughts?

When I was in year seven, I tripped down some stairs at the end of the school day and badly twisted my ankle. When I phoned my mom to tell her that I couldn't walk on it, she told me to phone my dad for him to come and pick me up. I called him, but unfortunately he was working and told me to take a taxi back to his house, which he would pay for. In retrospect, I should have done just that, but I was only twelve at the time and naturally felt like I needed to get my mom's approval first. She is quite volatile when things don't go her way. To her, the fact that my dad chose the 'easy option' of having me take a taxi as opposed to personally coming to pick me up, was evidence that my dad did not care for us in the same way that she did. It didn't matter to her that he was unable to do so because of work.

As such, she told me that I couldn't get a taxi and would have to get the train home. By the time I'd gotten home an hour later, my ankle had swollen to the size of an apple and I was in absolute agony. I still can't quite believe that my own mother had me travel home in agony simply because she wanted to 'prove' that my father had 'abandoned me' and would never be there for me in the same way that she was. I was on crutches for a couple of weeks.

There were several incidents where my mom had so much anger and resentment toward my dad that she would suddenly implode and use me as tool against my dad to 'show' him that he couldn't get away with behaving the way he was. My brother was at boarding school and so I bore the brunt of these episodes.

On one occasion, when I was in year eight, my mom told me one morning as I was getting ready to go to school that I was to go to my dad's that evening and that I was not allowed to come home. I knew that my dad was away on business, and told her this, but she did not want to hear it. Sure enough, that evening she wouldn't let me come home, even though I pleaded with her on the phone after school. I ended up having to spend the night at a friend's house and, at the time, that was quite embarrassing for me.

On another occasion, my dad was dropping me home after I had spent the weekend with him, and my mom was waiting with a pile of clothes that she wanted him to drive to my brother at school in Oxford. He told her that he didn't have the time to journey from London to Oxford and suggested she simply mail them to him. After he left, we got in the car and followed him to a red light on a busy main road and she gave me the clothes and told me to get out of the car. I had to run down the middle of the road to my dad's car. To her, again, the fact that my dad refused to travel to Oxford simply to drop some clothes off was more evidence of his 'neglect' of us.

One morning, completely out of the blue, my mom woke me up very early in the morning (perhaps around half past six) and told me to go to my dad's. I don't know what caused this particular outburst, but I was forced to walk from Richmond to Kew (1.5 miles) in my pajamas, without any money or phone, and with just my school books. She wouldn't let me take any of my things because 'she had paid for them and if he cared about me he should do the same'. Because I was still in my pajamas, I walked along the river which was still very quiet as opposed to me going through the busy town center!

How did this affect your home and school life?

My home life became extremely fractured and difficult. From a very young age, my mother would often ask me to leave and go to my dad's house or simply drop me off, wherever she knew he would be. My dad, who had remarried and I can only assume wanted to avoid conflict, would on most occasions simply drive me back home a few hours later. I was left feeling like I had no real home and no one to turn to when things got particularly bad, which they very often did. When I was twelve, following an argument between my parents, I was forced to leave the school I had attended for ten years and move to England with my grandparents for two years to finish sitting my English exams, so no part of my life was unaffected by what happened.

Were your friends supportive?

It's not something I felt comfortable sharing with my friends, particularly as all of my close friends' parents were happily married.

Did you keep your connections with all your family members and grandparents?

Yes.

Do you feel it was the right choice for them to divorce?

Yes. Sadly, they did not make each other happy and were simply not compatible as a couple.

If you could change two things, what would they be?

The first thing that I would change is the way my parents were unable to set aside their differences throughout and following the divorce and put on a united front for our sake, for the sake of my brother and me. The second is the way I was made to feel like an unwelcome guest when my father remarried and had more children; you don't divorce your children.

What have you learned about yourself from this experience?

That I am a very strong and self-contained person albeit slightly fiery at times! Growing up I didn't have anyone to turn to when things got particularly bad between my parents and it wasn't something I could discuss with my friends, so I had to learn very quickly how to manage and cope with these feelings introspectively. It is said that every cloud has its silver lining, and for me it's that I was able to develop important personality traits from a very young age that I think will hold me in good stead throughout my life.

If you could say one thing to your mother about how she handled everything, what would it be?

This is difficult for me to answer. I think that she handled the whole situation dreadfully and I very often felt like I wasn't her daughter but a tool she had at her disposal to inflict pain and revenge on someone she had very deep-rooted anger towards. But I also know that her behaviour was exacerbated by her mental illness and that when she was herself, she did the best that she could for my brother and me.

If you could say one thing to your father about how he handled everything, what would it be?

I would tell him that I know he did the best that he could in the circumstances, even if it didn't always feel like it at the time.

What is your relationship with your father like?

I enjoy a very strong relationship with my father. Over the years, there have been some arguments and some times where I felt like he could have done more to shield me from a lot of what I was experiencing and enduring. In spite of this, however, I grew very attached to my father from a young age and he has been a source of comfort to me for as long as I can remember. And, as I got older, he was someone I could turn to when I felt I had nobody else. I've also always never been afraid to truly be myself around him which is something I have always valued as my mom is extremely critical of me, from the way I walk, my introverted and solitary nature, to my weight etc.

What would you change about your parent's situation now if you had a magic wand?

I would just want to make sure that they are both happy.

Do you believe in marriage for yourself in the future?

Yes! I don't think it's healthy to mourn the past and I don't. I didn't have an ideal childhood as a result of my parent's divorce but the whole experience has helped shape the person I am today and I wouldn't change a thing. However, having never experienced a 'typical' family upbringing, I definitely want that for myself in the future when I start a family of my own.

What have you learned about adults from this experience?

I've learned that often it's all too easy to allow ourselves to be consumed by momentary rage, jealousy, indignation, etc and that we forget about what really matters and, also, that life is too short to allow ourselves to get caught up in petty arguments. Ultimately, the only people we end up hurting in these moments of impulse are ourselves and the people we love who get caught up in it all. In my parent's case I feel like both of them missed out on really watching my brother and I grow and develop into the people we are today and, in my case, I feel somewhat robbed of the idyllic childhood I could have had, had my parents put their differences aside and focused on what was really important – their children and simply enjoying life.

What's your relationship with your two stepsisters like?

Has it been hard watching the girls treated better by their mom than I was by mine? This is something that I am often asked but I can honestly say that I feel no animosity towards my sisters over the radically different childhoods we had. In fact, I had always wanted a younger sister (I was eight when my first sister was born and my older brother wasn't always very nice to me!) and for me, her birth was one of the happier times and one of the best things to come out of my parent's divorce for me! I've always enjoyed a close relationship with both of my sisters, despite the fact that we didn't always see each other often and I'd never want anything but the best for both of them, so no, seeing them treated better was not the hard part for me. What was difficult was how differently I was treated by my stepmom when I visited or lived with them compared with how she treated her own children. This was a source of constant tension, especially as my brother and I didn't have a place I could really call my 'home'. My youngest sister is twelve now – around the age I was when my own mother started throwing me out onto the street – and it makes me wonder, now more than ever, how an adult could have done that to someone so young and innocent and oblivious to what was happening around her. But – as I said before – I try not to focus on my past and instead focus on building the life that I want for myself now and in the future.

What's your relationship with your stepmother like?

When I first met my stepmom I thought that she was the kindest, most beautiful woman I had ever met and often dreamed of her being my mom. Sadly, things changed when she had her own children with my father and I started to feel like an unwelcome guest. I couldn't visit my dad apart from on his allocated weekends, despite the fact that I lived round the corner. I was never invited on family holidays whenever they went away, I had to refer to my mom as the 'm' word whenever I came to stay because my stepmom despised her so much (these are just a few examples).

Our relationship really deteriorated when my brother and I went to live with my dad, stepmom and sisters when we were about seventeen and fifteen respectively. The difference in treatment between us and my sisters became much more acute, now that we were all living under the same roof and – whether rightly or wrongly – we became very angry about the whole situation, especially towards my father who we thought didn't stick up for us enough. Now – staying true to my motto – I don't let what happened in the past define who I am today and have decided to simply move forward from all the negative feelings I was harboring towards her. It simply was not worth the energy and it also made seeing my sisters, and enjoying the time I spent with them at home, a lot more difficult which is not what I wanted for anyone. Now my stepmom and I really do enjoy a much closer and stronger bond than before.

INSIGHTS

I found Isabelle's story very compelling, particularly because I've known her for years. She's an incredibly beautiful young girl and currently studying to become a lawyer, to defend the defenseless and seek justice for those who can't do it for themselves. Despite her harrowing, emotionally lonely childhood, she found great strength in herself. Do you think because she had a somewhat privileged life that she didn't suffer any less than a child in a poverty-stricken home? You'd be very mistaken if you think so! Emotions are exactly the same no matter what the circumstances and some people forget this.

Money does not buy emotional happiness and a child in a situation that appears wealthy has exactly the same feelings and inability to cope as any other kid in the world. It's true. During my years as a children's nanny, counselor and clinical hypnotherapist, I have met with many kids from all backgrounds and their stories are identical in how they feel inside, so we do a huge disservice to those we feel are okay just because there might be more money around. In a bigger house with less interaction with a loving parent, it can be much lonelier for children and with little hope of emotional comfort.

Isabelle's first memory of her parents divorce is one of confusion; she even questions if her memories of the divorce are real. This is common in kids who have gone through trauma way beyond their tender years. Isabelle's mom forced her onto her dad many times. She humiliated her terribly, dragging her out of bed at six-thirty one morning and demanded she walk, in her nightclothes to her dad's home in the next town. It was winter, freezing cold in France, yet the rage and hatred towards her mother's ex-husband outweighed common sense and kindness. Her mother made her walk with no phone, money or school clothes just to appear at her dad's house so he'd be forced to take her to school and clothe her.

Another time she made Isabelle go to her dad's home after school even though he was away on business. Isabelle begged her mother to let her come home but she refused, causing more unnecessary shame and emotional abuse toward her daughter. What also was there to gain by making Isabelle get the train home after she'd sprained her ankle so badly? Was it to make her dad look bad and prove him to be a monster? No, her dad suggested she got a taxi, and he offered to pay for it as he was at work. But her mother chose to refuse this suggestion and Isabelle ended up having to walk on crutches for two weeks. What benefit was there for her mother to make Isabelle jump out of a car and run on a busy road at a stop light to make her dad take clothes to her brother at school, and finally forcing Isabelle to leave France on a whim, to get at her dad and send her to England for two long years?

It's a sad read but as well as a clearly cold cruel mother, remember that this mother was suffering from a mental illness. There is no excuse for deliberate cruelty but there are some parents who are so affected by a divorce and have to accept their ex-partner marry someone else and have more children. This can be mentally damaging. Perhaps in Isabelle's case her mother was mentally ill long before the divorce.

Isabelle shares with us that she loved her stepmom at first and fantasized that she would be her own true mother. When her stepmom had two little girls the obvious differences in how Isabelle was treated by her own mother, and her witnessing the loving safe home her sisters had with her dad was overwhelming.

I am fortunate to know her stepmother and I can tell you that this lady is one of the kindest sweetest people I have ever met. I remember her stepmom, Charlotte, worrying how to communicate with her stepdaughter and I saw her walking on egg shells around Isabelle many times. This is another common theme at times in blended families and is never an easy thing to get right. If Isabelle had had the courage to speak up in a way that she could have been heard, things might have turned out differently, but she was only a young girl living a traumatized life. If her stepmother had been able to address her feelings and been able to 'reach' Isabelle, that may have made their situation different, too. But Isabelle's dad was caught in between his ex-wife and new wife and that, for some, is a minefield. There is no blame here; it's just a sad situation that is all too common in divorce.

If we teach our kids at a young enough age that they have a 'voice', that they are safe and can express what they need to without fear, we would do them a great service. Isabelle dealt with what she had. Her father knew nothing of the real situation at her home with her mother; he only heard little bits here and there, and he truly thought he was doing the best he could at the time. We humans are hard-wired in our brains to believe that we are doing the best we can for our kids, but sometimes we simply fail to get it right.

Some kids hold anger and jealousy towards stepsiblings but how lovely to note that, despite her own childhood, Isabelle always loved her stepsisters and didn't let what she was going through harm her relationship with them.

CHAPTER SIX

EMILY, AGE 15, GERMANY

Emily is an adorable young teenager who was at ballet boarding school. She has a brother who is away at school too and a little sister who remained at home throughout her parents divorce.

How old were you when your parents told you they were going to divorce?

I was 15 years old, I still am and I live in boarding school and it was early last year, a week before I was due to go home on a school break.

How did they tell you or did you know it was going to happen?

The past year I didn't think they would be together anymore because they were too different. I hoped they would keep it together, but I had a feeling they would split up eventually. They told me over the phone when I was walking back from lunch at school; Mom told me they were going to separate. They had been together since college and were so young when they met and they had changed so much as individual people so many years later.

How did you truly feel about this decision?

When I first heard I was really angry, not so much sad. I was so angry at my mom because she was the one who told me and I thought she was the bad guy and my dad was the good guy and I was really confused. I thought that they would work things out but they didn't and I was surprised and upset at them and thought they didn't consider me, but later I found out that was not the case.

How did it affect you personally? What were your deep inner thoughts?

I felt that I didn't have a ground anymore like I had been torn into two pieces! I didn't want to go home or have anything to do with either parent. I called my dad and asked "Why would you do this? It's so stupid it's too hard on me as I'm away at school." I was so mad at them I thought it was stupid do this.

How did this affect your home and school life?

When I went home for break it was fine, it was more the awkward stage when they had just separated. The first two days my dad wasn't living in the house but he came to the house. My mom and dad were acting weird. It didn't feel right and I had an angry outburst. The second day, my mom told my dad that she wanted a divorce and I was really emotional and thankful I wasn't in between. I thought as they were together but not living together it was really weird. I asked my mom "Why are you doing this to dad?" and I told her I was confused. I said "Mom, he's all alone, he's far away and you have us all the time!"

But later on it was explained why this was for the best and their divorce was definitely going to happen. Dance school at the time was a distraction from everything and dancing helped. It was a gateway to get away from it. My sister is at home she's alone; she doesn't have my brother and I to support her and she's still going through things. I think sibling support is very important. Us three are all very close. I do get annoyed at my little sister, but we are there for each other. I really think all siblings should be there for each other while parents are going through something like this. We had secret talks and were there for each other as we were all in the same boat.

Were your friends supportive?

At first I would not tell my friends. They knew I was upset and they didn't know why. I kept saying I didn't want to go home and I was the girl that always looked forward to going home and I was always counting down the days and one day I didn't want to go home any more, so my friends asked me what was wrong and I told them. They were very supportive. One of my friends was going through it and another had problems in her family. My other friend told me her parents were separated and I realised that other kids go through it and as we spoke and shared I felt there were friends to go through it with me. It's funny what you don't know until you reach out and share. When you share it's good to talk about your pain as my friends understand, but even if they don't connect to a divorce or have not gone through their parents' divorce, they are good for smiles.

Did you keep your connections with all your family members and grandparents?

Yes. This if off topic but my friends and other people asked me if I hated my dad. I think that people take sides but later my mom explained to me they were not bad guys. Mommy said "If your dad did a horrible crime it wouldn't change anything." I still love my mom and dad very much and my feelings will never change towards them. With mom's side of the family I still connect to them. I'm closer to my mom's parents, but less with my dad but I know the sides are now against each other. But I know I can reach out to them any time, so I am actually in touch with everyone and I don't think the divorce will affect that. Family is family.

How did this affect you?

It was very emotional when it happened. I was already having homesickness problems, but when this happened it put the icing on the cake. It felt like I didn't have a family to come back home to, like it was all done and my parents were at war and sometimes it gets really hard as they slip and say something about the other parent and they get too close sometimes and they forget to be perfect. Both of my siblings have had a breakdown because there have been misunderstandings. Mom would say "Oh your father did this and this" and she would refer to different things, never bad things, but it felt wrong to hear her discussing him and I would say "You don't have the right to say anything about my father!" Even though she wasn't being unkind about him, it felt wrong, it didn't feel right. There was a time when me and Mom would talk about it and it felt right but in the end both my parents are happy and they can be themselves and they don't have to be a mob or arguing people. They are emotionally stressed and Mom doesn't have as much time for me lately, but they really care and I tell them it is just simply sad.

Do you feel it was the right choice for them to divorce?

Definitely it was definitely the right choice. I would never want my parents not to be themselves. They were not happy, either of them, and now they can do what they want and I believe they are supposed to be happy and they can start their lives again and I'm really happy for them. We had good years. It was not all horrible; we had great years. It was a breakthrough for me to understand.

My mom got out all her albums and showed me how happy she used to be. All the pictures of her are so happy, joyful and she was having fun and being free and then I thought "I want this for both Mom and Dad" and I thought "It's good it's happening." I know the divorce could have gone smoother, but it doesn't always work that way but that's ok because in the end it's all fine. The pictures were of her college time. She was a little girl my age, so pretty, and she was dancing having the same life as me and it showed me that she is not just a house mom who cooks, cleans and sweeps. She had a beautiful life and she deserves that. Same as my dad. There is one photo where he is laughing with his cousin and I thought it was a connecting point for me and I felt we could connect in that way to bring that back.

What is your relationship with your mother like?

We are a lot alike, not only look wise but we are empathetic and that's why they were married for so long, as they really care about people and they really care about us. We both have the same interests and socially we let people walk over us and let people take over us and we don't set boundaries and we don't speak up. I have yet to learn that and she is learning it now. She needs to go out knowing this is not the end she can have another life and explore, work and do her dream work and find what makes her happy. My mom was there from day one for my whole life. I don't remember a moment without my mom even though they are divorced. I know that she is just there; she has been there for my first melt down until I got my first pointe dancing shoes. She always put us first and now I'm happy she is putting herself first, as she really deserves that. I so love her, I tell her that so much I'm always texting her "Goodnight, Mom I love you so much" and many hearts as I'm still in boarding school. I do have separation anxiety but it's getting better.

I say the same for both of them. I love them both so much and want the same things for my dad and, even though he is more alone, he knows I will come see him. He worries that I won't and sometimes I find it hard to go back and forth and I try to please both sides and I want him to know that we all love him and he can do what he wants.

What is your relationship with your father like?

Me and my dad are hard workers. He always tells me, "Ever since you were in the cradle I would whisper in your ear, never give up". At school a lot of people get the answer right away and I have to work hard at that and every day he tells me never to give up and to work hard because anything is possible. He's never told me 'nothing' is possible. His word choices are so correct. Everything he says is so uplifting; he's very supportive. We are close. I definitely am Daddy's girl.

If you could change two things, what would they be?

I would change how ugly the divorce went. Some parents can go out of marriage as friends and I wish I could say that they would be friends but I know that I can't necessarily say that and I ask them "Do you think in ten years you will be able to have a conversation?" I personally hope they can as right now they don't know. My dad said "this is heart-breaking for me, too. Your mom was my best friend." Deep down they have gone through so much together; there is no way in ten or 20 years they will not be speaking to each other, as they loved each other so much. I tell them "I wish I could bring you back to the age you were at 16." I think everything happens for a reason and my mom says it's also a lesson for me. She wants me to know that I need to speak up, as right now I'm having trouble speaking up and I think she wants that for me. It's not that she didn't speak up in her marriage, but she wants me to be a strong woman. I think one of the big messages my mom is giving me is that as a woman, I need to stand strong and have my ground. I don't need to be dependent on anyone else and I believe my dad wants the same thing for me, too, to be a strong woman.

What have you learned about adults from this experience?

I think they both will work hard for what they want. They have a drive, I know that what they believe is true, and they will speak their opinions. Sometimes I wish they would be more adult about it and they need to leave it! Kind of get over it. I know it's hard for them; they probably both hurt in the process, but I hope they get over it and move on with their lives. My ultimate wish is that they can be respectable friends.

What have you learned about yourself from this experience?

Not really sure. I think I am still figuring that out, I've learned a lot. I think I should not make judgements or accusations as I blamed my mom, but then I heard what happened from both sides that they were fighting all the time and they were both unhappy and the divorce made sense. I think I will not let myself judge without knowing both sides first and I need to learn to be stronger and give a voice to myself. That's what I learned a lot as I've been quiet and I need to speak up as my own value is worth the same as everyone else and not any less.

If you could say one thing to your mother about how she handled everything, what would it be?

I would say I'm so thankful that I have a mother that is so strong and she told me "sorry if I wasn't that strong" and I said "Mom,

I can't believe you are saying that as even though you
happy you are the strongest person I know. I knew you wi
and so strong through the divorce that you can go into t
and do what you want and you are not just a house mom or a slave.
You mean so much more than that and I'm so happy that you took
this step forward and you can live your own life."

**If you could say one thing to your father about how he handled
everything, what would it be?**

I would say the same things he says to me, "Never give up. You're
a hard worker, you're the best dad in the world." He let me come
to this cool school where he worked day and night for me to do
what I loved and I think it's so great he can be in the world and
I his daughter look up to his strength, drive, perseverance and
hard work and I know that I can have that, too. He always used to
whisper in my crib and in my bed when I was older that I was a
hard worker and I could do anything I wanted and to never ever
give up. I like that he put that advice in me, as I never forget it and
I hear his voice in my heart.

**What would you change about your parents' situation now if
you had a magic wand?**

If I had a magic wand I would wish for them to have a clean divorce
one that was not so ugly it would be easier for them both and they
would still divorce but it would have been easier for them.

Do you believe in marriage for yourself in the future?

Oh, yes, of course. What I learned from what they have gone
through and if I get married, I know I'm still a person and can

stand on my own and if I do get married, I don't think it's out of the question as my parents were happy and that is what I remember.

What would you say to other kids and teens going through this?

The main thing I would say is to never give up and not believe that it won't be ok. I know it's hard and nothing can change but being hard makes you stronger and family stronger and even though your family is not together, it is still a family and that will never change.

UPDATE

Since my interview with Emily took place, she has been diagnosed with an immune disorder. Her life has completely changed once again. She has had to leave her beloved ballet school and is now home schooled and living full time with her mother.

What has happened to you since we last met?

Since the last time that we have talked a lot has changed. This summer I was diagnosed with Addison's disease, which is adrenal insufficiency. This took all summer and kind of brought my mind off the whole divorce.

How are you feeling since your diagnosis?

As of now, I am feeling wonderful. Some days it's harder but I feel at peace because this is a part of me that was trying to come out, and I am glad it did or I could have had a crisis. I am working on seeing an acupuncturist really soon to help myself feel better, because I'm a not one hundred percent sure how that feels like. For the longest time I never felt good and I thought that was normal, which it isn't.

What has changed since you left boarding school and got it into your home life?

I am much less stressed because I am finally back with the people I love and the people who support me and I love being back with all my pets! Something else that has changed is that I am now in the middle of the divorce, so I see it happening right in front of me, where as at school I wasn't really sure of what was going on and now I understand and see it much more clearly, which isn't a bad thing but not necessarily a great thing either. I get caught in other people's emotions and take them in, which is something I am trying to work on.

How do you feel about leaving school and moving back home?

It was really hard saying goodbye to such a wonderful community and such amazing faculty and students. One year may not seem like such a long time but it was a perfect amount, because I believe everything happens for a reason. It proved itself right because I then got diagnosed with Addison's where I wouldn't have been able to go back anyway. I am very thankful that I had this experience, but I'm glad to be back in the comfort of home.

How have your parents coped with the news, how are they treating you and each other?

My mom was there with me when I went through this process and helped me through it all and I'm very happy she did because I wouldn't be able to do it myself. She's always reminding me that this is my life plan and I am learning from it and that really eased my mind. My father knew that this was happening and gave me good advice but wasn't necessarily as supportive because of financial things and different beliefs. With that I wish he was more considerate, but he gave me a lot of emotional support because I am dealing with anxiety. My parents seem to not agree with anything but I have high hopes that this will get better. It's important to look brightly into the future.

Are they blaming each other for your challenge?

They haven't done that at all because they know that no one has any control over it and that it lies in the angels' hands. No one can prevent this disease, it happens to the few.

Are they working together more for you and your siblings?

My parents aren't usually on the same page, so it gets really hard making decisions. They always are opposite, which really stresses me out, but I just have to stay patient.

Have you seen a change in their attitudes to each other since you came home?

I think when I came home the divorce really fired up because they now have to make a lot of heath decisions and we always have to ask my dad for permission and that becomes really annoying because there used to be scarce heath decision making. Also it's hard because my dad always has a different opinion than my mom's and my opinions are similar to my mom's. It's important to respect other people's decisions but also to listen to them!

What would you like to say to your parents about this?

I would like to tell my mom to stop stressing and to look at the good things that are coming from this and to know that we all support her. And for my dad I would like him to think about me and what I feel is good for me. I would also say just to let it be, not to go against everything my mom says just to have the last word. I would also like him to know that we wont forget about him and that we still love him like we did before, nothing can change that.

What would you say to other parents in this situation?

To remember that the child still loves the other parent, even if you don't and that they need to know that that changes nothing about them and how we love you.

What and how would you advise other kids in the same position as you?

To stay positive; if one door closes, just open it, that's what doors do. Also smile!:) You are learning so much from this, which in the end will make you stronger.

INSIGHTS

Emily understood that her parents would divorce and that somehow made things slightly easier for her. She fully accepts that they met so young, when they were kids themselves and have changed dramatically over the years. She was told the news over the phone while at school and became angry at her mother, blaming her entirely. Thankfully she realised that it was a joint decision and there was no 'bad guy' to blame. So many parents stay together in silent misery for the sake of the kids, but kids always know. They are intuitive and feel and sense sadness in their parents. There is always a need for appropriate behaviour and it is never fair to a kid to be told too much information, especially negative private things that should stay between their mom and dad.

Kids often carry guilt that is not their own and they can at times take that into their own later relationships, causing a dysfunction and continuing a pattern of behaviours that were never rightly theirs to take on. The simple fact is that parents fare much better with their kids when they have good boundaries themselves. Unless the other parent is a raging lunatic and the child is at risk, they would do well to keep their negative thoughts towards the other parent "zipped' and not feed unhealthy information into their kids. The weight of the guilt bears heavily on a child who is already trying to figure everything out.

Emily talks about feeling that she had no "ground" under her feet to walk on. She felt torn into two pieces. She stayed close to her siblings and they had secret conversations to support each other. Some kids do the opposite and recoil from each other in non-supportive ways in an attempt to cope.

I loved that her parents showed Emily photo albums of themselves when they were young. Her mother had also been a dancer and Emily realised her mother had had a big life before having her and her siblings and that she deserved to have a full, rich "big" life again. Her father did all he could to keep her in her ballet school and he continued to after the divorce and before her recent diagnosis. He gave her strong morals telling her to always work hard for what she wants and be consistent. She knows her mother desires her to be a 'strong woman' and Emily feels that she has received much love and support from both of them.

Reading her update it's very clear that both parents are refusing to agree about her health care choices and that her dad is on a very different page from that of Emily and her mom. This causes more stress and, because her disease is stress-related, she has run out of adrenal support in her body for many reasons. Her life is again 100% different because not only has she had to leave her ballet boarding school, she is living back home and being home schooled. Could it be more of a drastic change for this young girl to be battling with disease as well as with her parents on going conflict with each together? She has lost her dream on all levels at this time. She, like all other children in situations such as this, deserves so much more. I want to wave a magic wand for this family to heal and the parents to find peace in their hearts.

There is a saying that you can only be as happy as your unhappiest child, so it's even more urgent that parents get on board to ensure the arguments and the relationship between them becomes stronger over time. Emily feels guilty for her little sister and protective of her and her older brother. So many kids carry unwarranted guilt and this could so easily be diffused and softened if the parents determined to let go of the anger and blame towards each other. That's easier said than done, of course, for some parents, but it's also so worthwhile and kinder on the children, many of whom suffer mentally and emotionally for many silent years.

CHAPTER SEVEN

JAVIER, AGE 17, U.S.

Javier is seventeen years old and an older brother to John. His biological dad left when Javier was five and he's not seen him since he was eight years old. His mom remarried and that father adopted Javier and his brother.

How old were your parents when they met and where did they meet?

I don't know where they met or how old they were. I have never asked.

How old were you when your parents told you they were going to divorce?

I don't remember the divorce, or them being together. After the divorce we did a lot of fun stuff with my dad. My brother and I would go to the local museums and his house near the ocean. He had a house with a basketball court. It was a big house. I remember the sound of his voice; he's from the south, I was five or six, and I know that I really loved him. When I was eight, my mom remarried and I don't really remember, but I don't think my brother and I wanted to see him at this point. He was out of our lives pretty quick and my new dad adopted me. I remember that we really liked our new dad and our real dad was not doing a good job anymore, so we stopped feeling so attached. There was a bunch of legal and court stuff that I could not understand, I don't remember a lot about that or think about it much anymore, I used to think about him but I stopped when he went away and Mom remarried.

How old were you when your mom and second dad got divorced?

I was fourteen, almost fifteen.

How did they tell you? Or did you know it was going to happen?

It was out of the blue, they just started fighting. I asked my mom if they were getting a divorce and she said "maybe". I was really upset because in my mind everything was normal. They did a good job of covering up their disagreements in general. My dad left for a couple of days and turned up to watch my brother's ball games. It was my mom that told me they were getting a divorce.

How did you truly feel about this decision?

I was upset. I thought everything was going to fix itself and they would work out their issues and take a break and work it out.

How did it affect you personally? What were your deep inner thoughts?

I was overwhelmed and upset and I didn't know what was going on. There was so much going on at the time it was like I didn't believe it was happening, but it was happening. I was sad, but as sad as I should have been, I was also in disbelief. It didn't really hit me that it was going on. I just thought everything would fix itself. My mom is a great fixer, she always gets things done and fixed.

How did this affect your home and school life?

My grades got bad around that time, but school was ok and everything was crazy. It didn't affect school too much, just my grades and I would think about their divorce a lot at school. Things were less organised; there was a lot more anger. My mom was going through a lot and things felt chaotic and overwhelming. My mom was great and she kept us in the house financially so we did not have to move. At the time I thought it was the greatest thing and a big deal, but now I don't feel we need a house this big and she had good intentions but worked way harder than she needed to.

Did you keep your connections with all your family members and grandparents?

We didn't see my grandparents too much on my dad's side. We are still really close with my grandma and uncle on my mom's side.

Do you feel it was the right choice for them to divorce?

I guess; I don't know. It wasn't really in my control. They did what they were going to do. Whatever they disagreed on was enough for them to not talk to each other in a friendly way anymore.

Did your parents meet new partners or remarry?

Mom had a boyfriend recently for a short while and Dad had a girlfriend who I never met. But they have not remarried.

What is your relationship with your mother like?

It can be good and sometimes bad, we argue a lot sometimes over stupid stuff. Sometimes I can be demanding and spoilt but I feel like I want to work arguments out. She will stay mad at me for a whole day and I like to work it out. She is a good person she supports us and works hard, she is caring and really cares about us. She is kind.

What is your relationship with your father like?

It's good we don't argue that much. We had disagreements at the beginning of the divorce. When we see each other everything is calm we usually have a good time. I see him every other week for a weekend. Sometimes, I want to stay at my mom's at my real home, though. Growing up he would sometimes get mad and really yell at me over stupid stuff, but he's got better about the yelling now.

He does not like my mom, and I feel like he tries to point out the good that my mom does to make us like him better, but he doesn't mean anything good he says about my mom. It's weird how he does it. I think he tries to get us to go on his side. I don't want to be like him in terms of him being divorced at his age; he also lives in a house near terrible schools. We talk, we get along.

If you could change two things, what would they be?

I wish I could understand more about what happened to make my mom and real dad split up. I was very young and confused and I wish I'd not been so young, as it felt like there was so much going on. It was overwhelming the second time mom got divorced; at the time it happened my mom was unwell with chronic stress and I wish the divorce had not happened then. Maybe if we moved to a smaller house, it would not be so hectic with all the bills.

What have you learned about adults from this experience?

They just get mad at each other and they do and say messed up stuff. Being mad has been a significant part of their lives; it seems the legal stuff takes up so much time and they spend so much time and money on it.

What have you learned about yourself from this experience?

I just deal with it, I got through it, it was really hard at times but other times I thought 'whatever happens, happens'. I feel like there were times I cared, but others when I was so overwhelmed I didn't care. I got used to it but it was still hard, I was not up in my room depressed I just got through it.

If you could say one thing to your mother about how she handled everything, what would it be?

She tried really hard to make everything good. She was really ill with chronic stress for a time. "I admire how hard you tried but I think you ended up having to work too hard in a time not good for you to work; there should have been another way. The situation was so bad but there was not much else you could do".

If you could say one thing to your father about how he handled everything, what would it be?

"Try to hang in there until after my mom got better. Wait a little bit longer until things calm down. Maybe you would have realized that it could get better, just pick a different time, work it out and realize a lot of different factors went into the way mom felt at the time of the divorce". She was going through a lot at that time.

Do you believe in marriage for yourself in the future?

Yes, I just don't want a divorce, as that would be really miserable for me, my wife my kids. It depends on the two personalities working things out together.

What advice would you give to other children to help them get through their parents divorce?

Don't have too many hard feelings against each parent until you're old enough to understand what really happened. There is no way you can't focus on it, but I deal with it. I didn't have a strategy I just deal with every situation. I was passive but that's because I had no power, or felt I had no power. I guess I would have a certain amount but not enough to make a huge change. I would tell my adoptive dad how I felt and what was wrong and at times I'd argue with my mom but for the most part, I dealt with it. Just go with it, it can be hard, but things do settle down. Every situation is different so things may not settle down, but my situation did and there are parts in all divorces that are similar.

INSIGHTS

Javier is a very tall seventeen year old and one of those kids that any parent would be proud to brag about. He seems destined for greatness in all that he does and has an air about him that makes a person feel that Javier just knows what to do for the best. I know his mother extremely well and she is one of the kindest, bravest people I've ever met. Javier is very like her and at times they clash, but he is her rock and he takes amazing care of his younger brother John (who you will meet in the next chapter). They are so incredibly close and have their own private dialogue. I have been at gatherings with them and no matter what the event, Javier and his brother are joined at the hip and do everything together.

Both have had two fathers and Javier's memories of going to the museum and the ocean with his real dad is sweet and sad to read as he's not seen his real dad for nine years. He remembers loving him and hearing the sound of his voice. Any fathers out there who think that they don't need to be a part of their kids lives and hope one day (especially in the case of Javier and his brother) that their sons or daughters will just find them are very much mistaken. I remember a very emotionally distraught father who came to my clinic telling me that he was certain that when his daughter was of a certain age that he could explain why he and his wife divorced. He was very wrong and learned the hard way that choosing to 'leave it up to the kid' can wreak terrible consequences for that child!

Javier seemed shocked at his parents divorce and it affected his grades, as he could not concentrate in school for thinking about what was happening at home. He hoped his mother would fix everything; she seemed to be the stronger parent in the home. He thought a lot about the divorce while he was in school and this affected his grades. Javier speaks of feeling guilty that his mother keeps him and his brother in a big house with all the financial responsibilities that go with it and feels that she shouldn't have to carry such a weight.

Clearly at age seventeen, Javier has experienced the loss of his two fathers from the family home and his main message to other fathers is 'to hang in there' if possible. It was a shocking time for his adoptive dad to leave his mom, who was going through treatment for chronic stress and this has affected him and his brother. There's not an easy way for anyone not to notice a personality flaw in that particular father and there are other parents in the world that have done and do the same. Do you think they actually understand the emotional damage they inflict on all concerned? How many of these kids grow up to have strong secure respectful relationships with a parent who 'ditches' them like this? Here's a hint: not many!

CHAPTER EIGHT

JOHN, AGE 15, U.S.

(Javier's younger brother)

John is fifteen years old and lives in California with his older brother Javier and his mother. John's real dad left when he was three years old and John has almost no memory of him. His mother remarried and his new dad adopted him and his older brother.

How old were your parents when they met and where did they meet?

They met when they were around thirty years old in San Diego. I don't know much about how they met. My mom was married twice but I don't think in terms of having two dads much at all. My first dad left when I was three, I don't remember him and my mom ever being together.

How do you feel about your real dad?

I never knew my dad. I don't remember anything about him really. It is messed up that he left! I don't think it was right for him to leave my mom. It would be good to talk to him. I don't know what I'd say. I wonder if he thinks about me. My mom told me a couple of stories about him recently; one was that he got kicked out of college but got picked up by Texas college to play basketball.

Another is that he bought her fake diamond earrings one time and she found out as one broke and she went to Tiffany's where he said he had got them, but the people in there told her they were fake! She called him on this and he said "Uh, Oh" then gave her his credit card details to buy new ones. She told me that they loved each other. They had to be in love to have me.

How old were you when your parents told you they were going to divorce?

I was three years old when my biological father left the house. I remember his apartment and that is it.

My mom remarried when I was really little and he adopted my brother and I. I was thirteen when they got divorced. He left and went to live with grandma, and he and my mom were separated for a while.

How did they tell you or did you know it was going to happen?

I suspected they would end up getting divorced. Dad moved out and I knew it was going to happen.

How did you truly feel about this decision?

I didn't like it. How could I like it? My parents were getting a divorce! This dad was a good dad to me.

How did it affect you personally, what were your deep inner thoughts?

I was sad for a little bit, then I just accepted it.

How did this affect your home and school life?

It didn't affect school, but at home it was different. My dad got a different house and we'd go visit him there. It wasn't too bad but his house was smaller. He lived with my grandma; she was nice. Sometimes when I would go there though, I'd miss my room and being home at my mom's house.

Were your friends supportive?

Yes, I didn't share too much at school. I just told a couple of good friends

Did you keep your connections with all your family members and grandparents?

We all kept in touch.

Do you feel it was the right choice for them to Divorce?

They could have waited until we were out of college, I would have preferred that. They argued a lot in the house. They didn't get along much. I guess it was good for them to get divorced.

Did your parents meet new partners or re marry?

They both met a couple of girlfriends and boyfriends. It's good; they should not have to be alone.

What is your relationship with your mother like?

Pretty good. She's nice and caring and a really good mother. She always tries to do stuff for my brother and I. She works really hard to give us a good life. I can talk to my mom about most things. She's pretty cool.

What is your relationship with your adoptive father like?

I feel like he tries to be a good dad; he tries to be nice. He is pretty nice to me and my brother. He's not a good 'business' person. He doesn't try hard to support us financially unless we are at his house. He gives us money to go out sometimes. He tries to support me emotionally but I don't feel I can tell him my secrets. He came to most of my football games before the divorce and after; I am glad he did.

If you could change two things, what would they be?

Maybe if Dad had stayed until my mom was healthier as she was very unwell at the time of the divorce. If they could be nicer to each other now, that would be good. If they stopped talking, then they would get along because when they start talking they always end up fighting!

What have you learned about Adults from this experience?

All adults are different. It's a different situation each time. I wouldn't have behaved the way my dad behaved and sometimes my mom was mad at me and my brother at the time of the divorce and a little bit after. My parents don't react right in stressful situations.

What have you learned about yourself from this experience?

I get through bad things by waiting it out until it gets better.

If you could say one thing to your mother about how she handled everything, what would it be?

"You did a good job during this situation. I probably couldn't have handled it if I was in your situation."

If you could say one thing to your father about how he handled everything, what would it be?

"You could have done better. I felt like you ran away from your problems instead of dealing with them."

Do you believe in marriage for yourself in the future?

Yes, I think I could do it. I would not get divorced unless the situation was really bad, but I'd try to make it the most easy on the kids. I'd wait until they got out of college or into college.

What advice would you give to other children to help them get through their parents' divorce?

Don't do anything stupid and just know that it will get better. Don't kill yourself; wait it out until things get better. Don't go out and do drugs because of a divorce. Don't do drugs and then tell yourself it's a way to cope with the divorce.

INSIGHTS

John is Javier's younger brother. He's very polite and, at just fifteen years old, stands over six foot three. As mentioned in the last chapter, these two brothers are incredibly close to each other and have what is called a 'twinning' meaning they have their own language and connection just between them and are fiercely protective of each other. Both their fathers left (the birth father and the adoptive father) and the brothers have not had many strong male role models in their lives to look up to. Their tight bond allows them to learn everything together, they have one another's back on everything and their mother is incredibly proud of the two men they are becoming.

John is very clear that he wishes his dad had left once he and his brother were at least in college. He mentions this twice in his chapter. It's impossible for some parents to wait out long unhappy years so, and there are other parents who do just that. In my experience, neither way avoids pain for the child and it would seem that it was healthier in John's case for his dad to leave as he found it hard to listen to the arguments. Did you notice that Javier was shocked at the divorce and thought everything was normal? It's amazing how different kids are in the same family, going through the same experiences but seeing and feeling differently about them.

It reminds me of Michael Jackson whose father admitted to whipping him on a regular basis. His dad treated his other brothers the same and none of them appeared to be as traumatized as Michael. Critics mocked his supposed 'weakness,' which to me is unjust. We can never know how a kid will react and it's not for us to assume they will be fine and not affected by parental behaviours. All kids are different in their ability to cope and the same kids in the same divorce situation often feel very differently from other siblings. They deserve the understanding and respect that it's ok for them to review their life in the way it is happening to them as they see it and not as a parent might choose to inflict or edit.

UPDATE

Since our first interview I am thrilled to report that John is back in touch with his birth father. Javier has access to him, too, and is waiting until he is ready to re connect. John has fewer memories about his real father but had a need to know who he is and all of his questions that had remained unanswered are being handled in a way that John can appreciate. The fact his real dad is back in his life is just incredible for him. So many kids lose a parent in divorce and many fathers just "ditch" them for years. They cannot possibly know what they leave inside their forgotten kids. Abandonment issues are rife in children with fathers and mothers who leave them. Years of torment, shame and emotional immaturity can and does, in some, ensue. At the ages of fifteen and seventeen, John and Javier need their father. It is said that kids age two and teenagers have similar emotions and need both parents more than ever!

CHAPTER NINE

SOPHIE, AGE 13, ENGLAND

How old were your parents when they met and where was that?

My dad was twenty-one and my mom was thirty. They met at the pub in the local village

How old were you when they told you they were getting divorced?

I was three, going on four. They didn't tell me they were getting a divorce until I was seven, and it was completely done. From when I was the age of three until seven, my dad slept on my mom's sofa at Xmas and at an apartment with a friend where he mostly lived in a local town.

How did your parents tell you or did you know it was going to happen?

I was at my Nan's house and they asked if I had realized they were divorced and I didn't recognize that they had at all. When I was going to school, I became sad that they were not together and at lunchtime I had a teacher who I would talk to and she would help me through it. I became nervous to answer questions in class during the time I realized they had got divorced. The teacher coached me over a four-year period and when I moved up to my senior school I was no longer in touch. She was really helpful over this time; she gave me confidence and made me, me again. Whenever I needed her, the other teachers would let me speak to her to get back on my feet.

How did you truly feel about this decision?

It was sad and, when I turned seven, my dad met another girl and they have been together for six years and she is like a stepmother to me and she is always there. We do have arguments sometimes but that is what happens in families. I can always talk to her when I need to, and if there is a problem at school, she will support me.

How did it affect you personally? What were your deep inner feelings?

I was happy they told me about the divorce when I was older so I could deal with it. I realized that they never really spoke to each other and they would go off for private talks but sometimes it would turn to arguments during the time they lived together. My dad moved out and they became more calm and it was calmer in the house. This went on for some years. About five months ago, my dad's girlfriend had a little boy who was born a day after my older brother.

When she told me she was pregnant, we were going on a camping trip and she asked me to be careful of her belly as she was pregnant. My dad called me and my brother into his bedroom and said he wanted to tell us something and he said Sue (his girlfriend) asked "Can we be careful of her belly?" and I was very confused, and then dad said "she is pregnant." Then I understood. On the outside I was super happy for dad and his girlfriend, but deep down inside that was the answer to all of my questions and I knew my mom and dad would never have a chance to be together again. It all came as a shock. I thought mom will be over the moon that dad and Sue had got this far but I didn't know to feel. I did not know how to feel or what I was supposed to do. Mom has always been supportive with dad and his girlfriend and has advised the girlfriend many times on how to handle my dad, so it was nice to handle the news on the baby.

How did this affect school and home life?

I don't know if this is connected, but I find it really hard to concentrate in class and I get angry a lot quicker than I used to and I find it hard to control that. The teachers tell me to control myself and concentrate but I find it difficult. On Sundays my dad would come to have dinner with us and he was always there on the morning of a birthday on the sofa, so he could wake up with us. When dad left it was calmer but more stressful for me and my brother as we had to prepare all of our school stuff as Mondays and Tuesdays we were at dad's house and Wednesdays, Thursdays and Fridays and every other weekend we were at our mom's.

I had a yellow teddy bear called Sunny and a yellow blanket called Blanky and these went everywhere with me, to mom's and dad's they were my little bit of hope. I still think even now at the age of 13 that I will get my greatest dream and that would be for my parents to get back together and even though I know in my heart that that might not ever happen, I still hope it will. Once at my dad's house I forgot to get Sunny and Blanky and I made my dad drive all the way back to get them as I had to have them near me all the time and would never be able to leave them behind and I was like that until I was 10. When I was this age, my dad got me another teddy bear that I could have at his house so I could leave Sunny and Blanky at my mom's house and that teddy was named "lotso hugging bear". He is a pink teddy bear that smells like strawberries and I always slept with him; I love strawberries, now they are my favorite things. My dad has been a comfort and when I am sad I think of Lotso and I think of my dad.

Were your friends supportive?

My best friend has been through the same thing, so she helped me and even now we talk about our parents divorce and help each other get through it. Sometimes if I have a bad day at school, I have a photo of my dad in my room and look at it. I look on the positive side and see how much happier my mom and dad are. I am a daddy's girl. I live mostly with my mum and I am happy with this. I have my own room. I love to do gymnastics and sing to express myself and I can do this freely at my mom's house as there is more space. Sometimes I have had situations where another kid has overheard me talking about the divorce and laughed and that makes me angry as I don't feel like I have a full family.

Did you keep all your connections with all your family members?

Yes, we have connections and my parents all get along with their parents so it is a good situation and my dad's parents just live down the road from my mom's, so I can see my grandparents anytime and at times after school when I get off the bus, I can pop into see them.

How did this affect you?

I feel really lucky as I know a lot of people whose parents do not speak to each other and I feel like I've been touched by the gods as I don't have to deal with any of that. My step brother is very cute and playful. I don't know if they will get married, his girlfriend wants to but I don't know if they ever will. I would be happy for them if they did but it would really crush me inside.

Do you feel it was the right choice for them to divorce?

I think it was because, if I look back at it now, they would not have been happy and the thing is right now my parents are happy. There was someone who liked my mom, but she explained that he liked her more than she liked him and I understand that Mom wasn't going to go for it.

What is your relationship like with your mother?

It is pretty good I would say. We have the odd argument the same as all kids. I have a great relationship, we have good days and bad days, some days we are as happy as can be and some days something will go wrong but we always make up. We have a saying that you can never leave the house unhappy, as you never know what might happen. Most children don't like their parents around if they are hanging out with friends, but if my friends don't want my mom hanging out, then they are not my friends I would not let friends get in the way of my relationship with my mom. She understands me and what it is like to get angry quickly and she understands my emotions.

What is your relationship like with your father?

Amazing. We always have a laugh. The only time we argue is bedtime because I don't like to go to bed. I think if I was to argue with my parents, I would lose my relationship with them and I don't want that. He is always there for me; he doesn't really care what goes wrong as long as we find a way to fix it. When he is in his garage, I will go in and help him fix cars. The other day he was welding a car and I put on a mask and I was on fire duty and we always high-five and it's epic.

If you could change two things what would they be?

I would probably go back in time and be nicer to my mom and dad because I was a bit of a naughty child and they were going through a hard time and I realize that now. I should have been nicer, so it would have been easier for them to cope with their break up and divorce. I wish I could turn back the clock and talk to my teacher that helped me when they first broke up and get back on my feet again.

What have you learned about adults from this experience?

Probably that even though when you think you know them they will always surprise you and even if they are going through a hard time they will always be there and don't ever take advantage as you only get two parents and you are never going to have any more. So, even if they do stuff you don't want them to just forget about it and keep going as you never know what might happen.

What have you learned about yourself?

Even when I think I am at my lowest I will always have a way to pick myself up, and I know now that I have more people to talk to than I thought I did and, as time goes by, I think stuff stays the same but it doesn't and it will get easier.

If you could say one thing to your mother about how she handled everything what would it be?

You did perfect, don't ever give up and if someone ever says you are doing it wrong don't ever give up as you are doing it perfectly.

She is a funny one. One minute she is happy la de dah and the next she can be sad, but there is always a way to cheer her up. I am proud of her for never giving up and for being her and not changing into someone else. Sometimes I say "oh this person's mom got her this" and I say "I wish I could have that." But I never want mom to change who she is or think that she is not doing as she is supposed to because she is. She is really strong and her own person and that makes her unique and that is good as if everyone was the same the world would be a boring place.

If you could say one thing to your father about how he handled everything what would it be?

"Well done for trying ". He slept on the sofa and comforted us and would do anything to make us feel at home. I see him as a "super hero" because this sounds a bit weird, but as soon as I am in need he comes straight to me. Even if he is helping others, he drops everything in the blink of an eye to help me.

What would you change about your parents' situation now?

I would change my mom being single. I would like her to have a man so that she has someone to comfort her. She once said Dad had it easier as he has a girlfriend. Earlier today my mom was saying that my brother bounces off her and I bounce off her but she has no one to bounce off or speak to about us.

Do you believe in marriage for yourself in the future?

I do, but if there is a divorce I believe there is always hope in the next one and you should never give up.

What advice would you give to other children to help them get through their parents' divorce?

Always look on the bright side and if something does go wrong always talk to your parents. Don't think you are going to do something wrong, because you are not and, if anything, you will be helping your parents as they are going to know what to do next time you need them. If you ever need someone to talk to the best person to talk to is a friend or someone you know you can trust to get advice on how to talk to your parents. Don't think you are doing it all wrong; don't blame yourself; don't think they broke up because of you as 99.99% it was not you, it was them not loving each other, which probably isn't your fault.

INSIGHTS

Sophie's parents divorced without telling her and her brother. They waited until they thought she was old enough and explained the divorce then. She seems evenly balanced about it now, but needed the comfort and support of a teacher who she was able to confide in over a long period. It's so sweet that she would love to see her mother with a man, so that she would have someone to comfort her. She speaks of her mom not having a man to bounce ideas, thoughts and feelings off. As sweet as it is, it's not her role in life to worry if her mom has someone to bounce off or not. But most kids want their parents to be happy so it's natural for Sophie to want to fix this.

In time her mom will most likely find a partner that suits her needs, but until then, she has her kids and Sophie feels empowered by this. I know her mother. She is a gorgeous feisty redhead who lives her life helping other kids in school and supports many parents in their daily child rearing lives. She is a strong example of giving her kids every spare part of her and Sophie's dad is a great guy, too, who has always made sure he's on the sofa, jumping up for her and her brother (who you will meet in the next chapter) for birthdays and Christmas as much as he can, despite the somewhat, at times, volatile communication between both parents.

Sophie has had a long time to build a safe bond with her dad's girlfriend and feels secure enough to know that her new baby brother is not a threat. She knows her dad loves her and there is no competition. For some girls it can be tougher to accept a new woman in their lives but it's clear that her dad's girlfriend had formed a strong trusting bond with Sophie before the baby came.

How clever of Sophie to find a teacher she could depend on! Most teachers these days have more than enough to deal with to add a dependent child of divorce into the mix; but there are some great teachers out there who go the extra mile for kids like her.

Sophie latched onto two special things when she went to and fro between her parents' homes. Her teddy and her baby blanket. This is common in young children and eventually her dad got her another teddy to keep at his house, one that smelt of strawberries a fruit she really loves to this day. Smells are deeply remembered by children and for her it brings back happy, safe feelings and memories. Her parents are a good example of life after divorce and clearly both made the effort to make their children feel loved all the way through, so much so that when a new little brother came to her dad, she was accepting. It meant that her parents will never get back together again and this was her deepest dream (as it is for most kids and some parents). I had a fourteen-year-old girl in my clinic one time who was bereft that her parents were divorced. When her dad met a new girlfriend, she was angry, volatile and did her best to come between them. It didn't break the relationship, but her behavior did put a strain on it. The girlfriend came to me, also, for counseling. She really understood how difficult it was for her boyfriend's daughter to want him to reunite with his ex wife. This thirteen year old was lucky to have such an understanding woman in her dad's life. There are many parents who thrust guilt on their kids when their ex's move on with other partners. Whatever happens, the kids should (in my opinion) be allowed to honestly voice their thoughts, at least flush out issues in the early stage, so they can be addressed and the kid can have an easier time accepting a new person in their family life.

CHAPTER TEN

SNOOP, AGE 15, ENGLAND

(older brother to Sophie)

How old were your parents when they met and where did they meet?

I think they met when mom was working in a bar and dad went in there for a drink. He was around twenty when they met.

How old were you when your parents told you they were going to divorce?

I was five.

How did they tell you or did you know it was going to happen?

First they didn't tell us immediately and they argued a lot and they actually didn't tell us until after they divorced. They still made sure that we saw them both as much as we could.

How did you truly feel about this decision?

Because they told us after it happened I felt kind of helpless and that I didn't have a say in it even though I was five. The arguments made me feel the worst as I was scared of the arguments. I remember one time they took an argument outside and I could hear it from the living room over the sound of the TV!

How did it affect you personally? What were your deep inner thoughts?

I think some of the time I felt it was my fault and at times I knew it wasn't, but it didn't stop me from feeling that way. I play back in my head what happened in the last days to see if there is anything that I had done to cause the divorce. I thought back to see if I had misbehaved. I honestly didn't know whether I had caused them to divorce. It took me until I was about seven and it was explained to me (as my parents sat me down) and let me know that it was nothing I had done. I felt relieved that I had nothing to do with it.

How did this affect your home and school life?

Nothing changed at school, but at home it was weird not having dad around as there was no routine. It was weird seeing him Sundays and not having him around the house. They have a lot of care for us and focus on making us happy and feel good and being able to have both parents.

Were your friends supportive?

I didn't really tell my friends until later on in life and they were supportive. I was around nine when I started speaking about the divorce because I didn't want to think about it.

Did you keep your connections with all your family members and grandparents?

Grandparents live close by and now that I am getting older I realize how special they are to me, but on the other hand I haven't kept in touch with other relatives such as my auntie or close family friends that we used to have, we just never spoke ever again.

How did this affect you?

I remind myself that if they really missed me they'd put in the effort to see me or talk to me but if they are not going to put the effort in to see me or talk to me I don't see why I should make the effort. I feel sorry for the kids that are going through divorce, as they can't change what their parents are doing.

Do you feel it was the right choice for them to divorce?

Definitely. They would argue all the time and I didn't like that.

Did either parent meet anyone else since the divorce?

Dad met his girlfriend five years ago. It was different having this new person about but he explained that she wasn't trying to be a mom or anything. She was a friend at that point. At first I was skeptical and nervous as I didn't know what she would be like, but she is very understanding and we have a good relationship. She got pregnant, but didn't tell us for a while. I was on a map holiday with my dad, younger sister and her and she kept saying she was feeling sick. They finally told me that she was pregnant. I was fourteen and I was happy for them. I knew she really wanted a kid. I didn't worry about my mom's feelings as she and the girlfriend get on well. I wasn't bothered about the baby because I knew nothing would really change in the family.

What would you say to other kids whose parents are having more kids with new partners?

Don't worry about it; nothing is really going to change. If anything, it will probably get better. Because I am older and more mature I realize that my dad loves all his kids equally and wont treat any of us differently. I love my new brother. He's part of my life and I can't wait until he grows up so I can form a bond with him. If one of the parents gets a new partner, my advice is don't worry or jump to conclusions. Me and dad's girlfriend get on really well, and at first I was wary, but after a time I saw she wasn't that bad and it was better as I just had to get to know her and give her a chance. She is trusting, I trust her. I used to get into a lot of arguments with her and over time I realized she was a nice person and there for me and she became an active part of my family.

What is your relationship with your mother like?

Not very good since last year. She stopped listening to me as I got older, I thought she didn't respect me and so now we argue and don't seem to see eye to eye. There are countless times I have had to stay at a friend's because I have been in an argument. She forgets I am an adult; she doesn't want me to get the train and go out with my friends and she is dictating what I can and can't do. She definitely always tried to be there for me as much as possible and tried to help as much as she can. She always tried to be the best mother that she could. She never had very much money, but she always tried to give us as many opportunities in life as possible and tried to take us on days out to Lego Land and that kind of thing.

What is your relationship with your father like?

That is quite good. My dad listens to me and he treats me with respect. He lets me go out and encourages me to find a way to get there from one town to another. I cycle a lot. Dad has always put in the effort after the divorce. He made sure he saw us. Sometimes we argue, but that is over schoolwork and what I plan to do with my life. A lot of the stuff I learn in school I don't know why I need it and, because I don't know what career I want, I am not sure what to learn to help me in life. A lot of my friends seem to know but I honestly don't have a clue what I want to do right now. It's hard, I don't know how I am going to get there or what path or courses to do. I don't feel motivated to do anything right now and sometimes I can lay in bed all day. I am not motivated to start a task or finish a task or get going at that time. This is where I am at. Dad just wants me to do the best I can in life and not drop out, as he got kicked out of school at fifteen and mom left school with no real qualifications.

If you could change two things, what would they be?

They work independently to help and support me, but I want them to work together as they say two different things. Ideally I want them to get on but they still argue. If it wasn't for me and my sister, I don't think they would still be friends.

What have you learned about adults from this experience?

Personally I don't like them. I don't trust them and I want to live my own life and I don't always listen to them. I think other kids should turn that around and form a friendship with them. I only really trust one person in my life and that is my dad's girlfriend.

What have you learned about yourself from this experience?

Probably that I am open about things and I will say things as they are. I tell the truth as I see it. I have changed my thoughts. I used to think divorce wouldn't happen to me, but it did and now I try to help others going through it. I would tell them it's not their fault and don't feel bad about yourself.

If you could say one thing to your mother about how she handled everything, what would it be?

That she did a good job. She explained everything all the way through and she was determined not make me to feel bad about the divorce.

If you could say one thing to your father about how he handled everything, what would it be?

I would say "thank you" for how much he stayed around and tried to see us as much as possible.

What would you change about your parent's situation now if you had a magic wand?

They would argue less because I feel like the middle man breaking them up all the time and I can't be bothered to deal with them, so that's what I would change.

Do you believe in marriage for yourself in the future?

Ideally I would like to as I'd like a family of my own, but I can't see it happening as I don't have a high opinion of myself to be honest.

What advice would you give to other children to help them get through their parents divorce?

My advice would be to talk to someone, and let them know how you are feeling, and always try to tell your parents if you can. Take a moment out of their day to let them know how you feel and how much it means to you and what impact they are potentially having on you and what the parents could do to help their child.

INSIGHTS

Snoop is a great character and full of good humour and at fifteen, clearly believes himself to be an adult. In England kids leave school at sixteen and either go onto further education or work. It is clear when reading his chapter that he sees himself as a man and longs for total freedom in his life in all areas. He clashes with his mother more probably because he lives full-time with her and he is the 'man' of the house and has been in this role for many years.

He worried for a while when he was much younger that the divorce was somehow his fault and struggled internally with this. His parents explained to him early on that it was nothing he did which greatly eased his mind. As he got older, he learned to protect his feelings in particular with family members whom he no longer saw on a regular basis. He decided that if they could not make the effort with him, then why should he bother?

A main point in Snoop's chapter is the fact that he feels like (in his words) the man in the middle' when his parents argue. He seeks guidance from both and wishes they were both on the same page as this is confusing for kids, when one parent says one thing is ok to do and the other parent wont allow it. It's kinder to work at this, to put the kids first but not all parents are willing or able to do this.

CHAPTER ELEVEN

CHARLOTTE, AGE 19, U.S.

How old were your parents when they met and where did they meet?

They were both twenty-three years old and met at a party. My mom was there with a boyfriend of six years and I think she was engaged to my dad six weeks later.

How old were you when your parents told you they were going to Divorce?

I was fifteen. My brother was 18 and leaving for college five days later. I was left alone.

How did they tell you? Or did you know it was going to happen?

No, it was a complete surprise and they didn't tell me together. I had a babysitting job that day and my mom was acting strangely in the morning. When I got home at five p.m. she was laying on her bed and she told me that dad was gone and he was having an affair with one of his students. He is a college professor. I don't remember everything she said— just that it was weird that she was laying on the bed at five p.m. in the afternoon. She threw him out of our house the next day.

How did you truly feel about this decision?

I think I was in so much shock. I never had a close relationship with my father; it was always clear my brother was the favourite and the only child he took an interest in so I didn't miss him. It was scary because my mother was not acting like my mother and my brother was leaving a few days later and all I kept thinking was that if my dad had been hit by a car and died, I still would have had a dad and I could have mourned him as my father, but instead what he did just made him a monster in my eyes. I was not close to him but I was always seeking his approval, which I rarely got.

Most times when we were all at the dinner table together, the game was how many times my brother and father could roll their eyes at me and belittle me making sarcastic cracks. It wasn't extreme; it's just that it was consistent and it made me feel small and made me feel less important.

I talked to my mom about it once and she said, "I never felt you noticed". I felt I didn't have the right to stand up for myself.

How did it affect you personally? What were your deep inner thoughts?

I felt so much shame for his actions. My mother made it very clear that I was not allowed to tell anyone, the neighbours or anyone. I grew up in an upper class neighbourhood and she didn't want to be the local gossip. I had no one to talk to about it. Mom always said that I didn't understand and that I have my whole life ahead of me. On a personal level, I almost claimed his actions as my own. I felt the shame he should have. And I was worried about what my friends would think of me if they knew I had a really bad dad.

How did this affect your home and school life?

Oh, god, it was dreadful. For the next two years, my father moved in and out of our house a total of ten times. My mom had a very tough time of letting go and seemed to be fighting a battle that was already lost. I hardly spoke to him the times he moved in. He didn't make any effort to talk to me, other than the very first time he moved back in with us. I ended up moving out of the family home on the final time he moved back in. I moved in with my grandmother. My entire life my mom talked about how lucky we were to be in the family we were in. All of her friends thought she had the very best marriage and she always talked about how happy she was with him, with us, with the house and she tried so desperately to get that back.

As much as she talked how she loved my father, she always had said she loved me and my brother more and she would always choose us first. When Mom told me the last time that he was moving back in I said to her "It's him or me" (because she had told me all of those years that I would come first, so in my mind I thought he wouldn't be coming back.) She just looked at me and said "Where will you go?" I grabbed my blow dryer, a change of clothes, a cosmopolitan magazine— and I was at my grandmothers within the hour.

We got on great; she was very motherly. My mom doesn't know how to cook and never did, which is not a bad thing but my grandmother is a good cook and I went to school with homemade lunches and had scrambled eggs in the morning instead of a pop tart. We spent almost every evening drinking tea and talking about life. I did talk to my mom every day when I lived at my grandmother's, but I didn't talk to my dad.

At school no one really knew what was going on. I was a really sad kid and a really good actress. My grades didn't drop and I was insecure like a lot of girls. I had no idea I was liked or popular, because inside I felt like I was falling apart but outwardly I looked like I was holding it all together.

Were your friends supportive?

My very best friend from kindergarten knew. Our mothers were also best friends. We didn't really talk about what was happening at my house but I spent every Friday night after school and all day Saturday at her house. It was a great retreat, we had a routine, certain TV shows, laying in the sun the next day, just girl stuff and it was great to know someone knew and I didn't have to talk about it.

Did you keep your connections with all your family members and grandparents?

Yes, with the exception of my dad. I am extremely close to my youngest uncle and he made a point to come and see me a lot and call me a lot. I have a lot of family in town and nothing really changed except that my dad was gone.

How did this affect you?

I think in my mind he needed to be gone; he didn't deserve us or a second third or tenth chance. What affected me more was how it changed my mother. When she started dating again, I would come home and she lost a lot of weight and she would be trying on my mini skirts and school clothes and I thought she looked ridiculous trying on my fifteen-year-old outfits. She was just not the mom I grew up with.

My dad left my sophomore year (I was fifteen) and, by my senior year, my mom was reunited with that boyfriend she had when she met my dad. It was a long-distance relationship and they were engaged within six months. She was travelling every other weekend for ten days and I was left alone. I had been accepted to a university writing program, it was a high end program and the night before we were leaving (and it was supposed to be for the whole summer) I came down with a terrible case of chicken pox. We didn't know I was going to be that bad and by the time we arrived at campus I was covered in the pox. I needed to go bed. My mom said her fiancé was going to be at the airport and she worried that she would not be arriving, she could not get hold of him as she forgot her phone and I didn't have his number. She had missed the flight by the time we got home. I think she stayed at home for one hour then she left and she went to see him for ten days and didn't call and I was sicker than I've ever been.

I don't think she realised how sick I really was. My eyes swelled shut; I couldn't see. I had 22 chicken pox on my right eyelid, but the point is she never called to see how I was and that was not like her. She was not a person who didn't care that her kid was sick. No one came; I was alone I couldn't even dial on my phone. Everyone assumed I was at college camp for the summer, no one knew I was really sick at home by myself all that terrible time.

Do you feel it was the right choice for them to divorce?

Oh my gosh! Absolutely.

Did your parents meet new partners or re marry?

They both did. Mom remarried her high school boyfriend for four years until he died of cancer this year. He was diagnosed a day before their wedding. He had battled it for years before they got back together. My dad still calls mom every day and six months ago they went to Thailand together, even though she was remarried. She can't seem to get over my dad.

My dad's affair didn't last and I think he just has girlfriends, but I've never met any of them.

Did you get stepbrothers and sisters? If so what is that like?

I got two stepsisters from my mom's new husband and I have only met them a few times. They were not at the wedding and I met them at summer break visiting my mom; they are much younger but we didn't do much together. My mom's husband had a very bitter divorce and the girls were very conflicted about their relationship with their dad. I don't think they were very close to him, although he was a very devoted father. He would drive four hours in the snow every week to see their sports games and, when my real dad lived in my house, he never came to see my games or my school plays or attended my high school graduation.

Did either parent go onto have more kids?

No.

What was your relationship like with your stepfather?

I really liked him. I didn't love him like a father but he was one of those overly positive sing-song men and it was hard to take him seriously. Everything was wonderful and fantastic and he was really a nerd but they married as I was going to college, so my only interaction with him was during breaks. But he was a good man and he loved my mom.

What is your relationship with your mother like?

It's great now. Those were the dark days when she was not herself, but she is really a good mom always thinking of others and not just herself and would do anything for her kids and friends. She just went a little nuts for a while.

What is your relationship with your father like?

Um … it is very strained and very formal. We usually have dinner once when I'm in town on a school break. He calls once a week or two weeks in college to check in. If we have dinner out in a restaurant when I'm home, he doesn't introduce me as his daughter. He didn't go to any graduations. He didn't help me move into my college dorm. He makes excuses so that he doesn't have to see my uncles and grandmother.

If you could change two things, what would they be?

If I could change anything it really would be that dad was never ever going to stay; it was never the perfect marriage my mom believed it was, so I would change the fact that my mom tried for so many years to earn his love. Even though she remarried, she still seeks his approval. I wish she didn't go through that as it hurt me too. It hurt to be second for so many years. It wasn't fair that I couldn't talk to people about their divorce apart from just my grandmother and one friend, I think it would have helped me not feel so ashamed of everything.

What have you learned about adults from this experience?

That they don't know every thing and that they are human, that their insecurities are not unlike my own as a college student. You grow up thinking that your parents always know more and set the right example and you don't really see your parents as human beings. That's what I've learned. They have the same flaws, same insecurities, same everything.

What have you learned about yourself from this experience?

I've learned that I need to catch myself often to stop still trying to be the pleaser. My entire childhood, even before they divorced, I was always feeling that I needed to please or be the easy kid. The one that didn't make any waves, and I still do that. I think knowing that I deserve more and actually going after that—those two feelings have not quite met yet.

If you could say one thing to your mother about how she handled everything, what would it be?

I wish she had chosen herself and I wish she had chosen me.

If you could say one thing to your father about how he handled everything, what would it be?

Just that he never deserved us in the first place and he still doesn't. He should have done better. Au revoir, goodbye, he just doesn't mean anything to me anymore.

What would you change about your parent's situation now if you had a magic wand?

I would absolutely erase all of the years between when she found out about the affair to the present day of still needing him to be in her life. I would take all of that away from my mom, so she could have moved on more quickly. I wish I had given myself permission to be really angry and call them out on their behavior, but I'm always trying to please.

Do you believe in marriage for yourself in the future?

Yes I do, I absolutely do.

What advice would you give to other children to help them get through their parents' divorce?

I think that they have a right to be heard, that their voice is important and that what they are feeling and experiencing is no less significant than what their parents are going through and should any of them be told, as I was to say nothing, not to listen but to find at least a few people that they can talk to truly and safely and say anything to. They need to be supported; that was the hardest part for me. I did have my grandmother, but I needed some of my peers. I needed people my age that have been through this. It would have been nice if it didn't need to be a secret! So my advice to kids is: "Don't suppress your feelings; do be heard; express yourself, even if it's not what your parents want you to say or to hear, but know that it's ok for you to have an opinion and be effective".

INSIGHTS

Charlotte is a very bright bubbly nineteen year old. She knows exactly where she is going in life and has big goals that she is convinced she will achieve. Her parent's divorce was harrowing and confusing to say the least. Her mother totally changed personalities for some very important years during the break up. Almost from the day her mom told Charlotte about her dad's affair, she acted in ways not 'normal' to her daughter.

Charlotte's mom had always told her and her brother that they were lucky to be in 'that family' and her mom believed she had the perfect marriage. Charlotte didn't feel the same when her parents were married because she dreaded dinner at the table, knowing that her father preferred her brother over her as he made it abundantly obvious by constantly making fun of her. She grew to think that what she had to say was not important.

Her mother also always told her that she would put her and her brother first, no matter what. You can imagine the shock when her dad had moved back in and out of the family home nine times and, on the tenth time, Charlotte told her mom to choose between her and her dad. Her mom chose her dad over her and the effect was devastating. Thank goodness, she had her grandma to live with and feel safe with. Charlotte would watch her mother try on her teenage girl clothes and try to act younger than she was, which was embarrassing to her. When she got chicken pox she had so many they covered her entire body and forced her eyes closed and she was left alone for ten days to cope because her mom did not call her once during this time. Instead, she chose to see her boyfriend and again Charlotte felt worthless.

There are many aspects to this chapter that touch areas in a child that can be hard to recover from, but despite this, Charlotte has somehow found a strength within her that moves her forward to focus on her own life independently. It is a shame that her mother felt the divorce details had to be a secret as all kids need a person, especially their peers, to share their fears and questions with. However in Charlotte's case, she respected her mom's wishes and stayed silent. Her relationship with her dad right now is non-existent, and she feels that it will remain this way as he was not there for her, he didn't support her and she doesn't trust him. When I asked her what would she change if she could she answered "I wish my mom had chosen herself and I wish she had chosen me". To this day her mother is still trying to gain the approval of her ex-husband, despite remarrying and now that her second husband recently died, she still has a need for approval. What does this say to a kid when a parent is unable to cut loose from a divorced spouse? It shows a lack of self worth in that parent, which is sad on so many levels. As much as we may feel we have the right to judge others, it can be tougher than we can ever understand for some adults to completely break away from each other. Divorce is rarely easy for any parent to cope with.

DO THE RIGHT THING

All the kids in this book are from different countries, races, religions and financial situations. The consistent similarity in all of them is the nature of their emotions. It doesn't matter whether a kid is living on welfare or in financial heaven. They all feel the same emotions and are equally powerless in their parent's decision to divorce.

All parents have a duty to their children to do what's right by them and for them. They signed up for this and there is no dodging it. If you are an aunt, uncle, grandparent, stepparent or influencer in a child's life, then you have a responsibility to do right by them. In every case your duty is not to inflict your personal feelings on them towards their mom or dad.

It's tough enough for a kid to know their parents might not love each other anymore—and it's not their job to carry guilt on their parents' behalf. What we largely see in society is divorced fathers having less connection with their kids than divorced mothers. There is a generation of dads who 'ditch their kids' and the consequences of this are painful and long-ranging.

A father came to me once in my clinic who had particularly unkind thoughts about his ex-wife. He blamed her for everything wrong in his kid's lives. He decided that she stopped him from seeing his kids, and, when he did see them, they played up, they were rude and he had no control. He thought that he would just leave his kids alone and hoped that one day they would seek him out and he could explain what went wrong. Guess what? That day never came and he left his children lonely for so many years that they just assumed he didn't love them and that they were not worth the effort. When they reached a certain age, they wanted nothing to do with him. They had done just fine with their one consistent parent.

This father didn't show up at school plays, he didn't send gifts as he thought they'd never get delivered to his kids. He never financially supported them in any way shape or form. He wasn't smart enough to find a mom at his kid's school, a teacher, a headmistress, or a mutual friend or family member who could give his gifts or relay messages to his kids. He believed that he could just explain away the years and tell his story that he was doing what he thought was best and could never communicate with their mother.

News Flash: Going through life making the other parent responsible for your kids' lives is no reason to not be in their lives or see them. If you have one child or more, you have a duty to financially and emotionally support them in whatever possible way you can.

Think about what your absence says to them. It translates that they are not worthy of support, financial or emotional. Even if there is a strained relationship both parents need to remember that they are the first male and female role models in their children's lives.

In England when a father walks away from the mother she can claim Child Benefit (financial support); studies suggest such fathers are ditching their kids because they know the state will look after them and they don't have to. Some moms behave just as badly and 'ditch'. Children are hard wired in the brain to love both parents.

There are always exceptions to this rule whether it is a mom or a dad because some people just don't know how to raise a child and, in extreme circumstances, there are some who should not be allowed to raise children at all. However, for the majority, the parent's marriage breaks down because they have fallen out of love with each other. The kids involved do not deserve the fallout that can come from this and they certainly do not want to hear how each parent might speak negatively about the other. There are mothers, grandmothers and other family members who behave just as abhorrently and I shall come to them.

Another father consistently mocked his daughter's mother for years. He was verbally cruel about her. He also thought that because he lived in a wonderful house and her mother lived in a poverty-stricken area, that his daughter would choose to live with him over her. This never happened and one day when this sweet shy little girl turned twelve, she chose to never see her father again. She is twenty-three now and doesn't regret it.

I knew her when she was three years old. She would always poop in her underwear when she was with her dad. This is deemed to some child psychologists as a sign of anger, and it drove him crazy. He would blame her mother for not potty training her correctly.

This child never had accidents when she was with her mother. From the age of three she was unable to cope with the hatred her father showed toward her mother and she never got over how many times he was disrespectful to her mother in front of other people and humiliated her in the process.

I have met with mothers in my clinic who are so full or rage towards their ex-husbands that they are intent on creating as much upset as possible in their ex-spouse's lives. A particular mother comes to mind. She had two boys and set up an arrangement with her husband that she would tend to the home full-time and he would bring in the money. For years, she would berate him for working long hours and when he would come home, the house would be a complete mess and she would have spent the day at the gym and lunching with friends. Her husband would be expected to cook dinner every night because he was a good cook. This mother was very mean verbally in front of her kids. Her two sons copied her behavior and treated their dad the same way their mother did. Total disrespect continued for many years and the dad felt helpless. One day he chose to leave the mother and hoped dearly that he would continue to build his relationship with his two boys.

The mother was determined to punish the dad for leaving, and it has been more than eighteen months since that particular father has seen his sons. He ended up living in a house with two elderly people in an effort to financially support his wife and kids in the lifestyle they had become accustomed to. He completely broke down mentally and emotionally because his sons would not see him, and it became clear their mother was deliberately preventing them from seeing him. This father works six days a week to pay as much as he can towards his sons' well being and has very little for himself. Parents break down! Some are so affected by a divorce that they are unable, for a time and sometimes a very long time, to recover.

It's so crucial that both parents try to maintain their child's emotional needs at all times but particularly during and after a divorce. Using kids as a tool to hurt the other parent is harmful in all ways. The father I am sharing with you is a really good guy. He loves his boys and he hurts every day he doesn't see them. He has cut himself off from friends and social events in an attempt to send money to support his kids and his ex-wife's lifestyle. This is a common theme in some divorces.

I am divorced but I am lucky that, even though at times I have got very annoyed towards my ex-husband, I know that he loves our children. He remarried a good woman. I have had to understand that, whatever my own feelings were towards him that if I am negative about him to my children, this hurts them and harms them emotionally. They cannot carry or mimic my own personal feelings, it's not their job!

At times I have enjoyed Christmas and other gatherings with my ex-husband and his new wife. What a joy this has been for my own kids who have come to learn that divorce is not always the end of their parents' participating in special times and family celebrations. I still, at times, behave in ways that I need to correct. I am human as we all are, and I, too, make mistakes. However, I try to be conscious and get my own self out of the way in order to create a healthy happy environment for my kids so they see that a good outcome to divorce is possible.

Kids grow up to hopefully fall in love and marry. Imagine how many have to deal with the selfishness of parents who may not be able to tolerate being in the same room as an ex-spouse? It's not the kids' role to carry the guilt or worry. I have seen far too many kids deeply hurt by parents, thinking of themselves first during times of special events, birthdays, holidays, etc. It is not always possible, of course, but the kids should be the priority.

It's time for adults to do the right thing. If you are preventing your kids from seeing their grandparents because you don't like your ex, then what level of emotional damage are you projecting onto your children? I agree that a law giving loving caring grandparents the ability to continue seeing their beloved grandchildren would benefit so many kids who miss out on these deep connections. Parents divorce each other and not both sides of the family. Of course there are always exceptions, some people are just unfit to care for kids; however, most are and want to continue being in touch with their loved ones.

Let's raise this generation of kids with unconditional love and understanding. It's completely possible and they can show you how to do this! Listen to them. Really deeply get to know them. Watch how they love unconditionally until they are programmed and taught not to. We will heal the pain when we recognize our chance as humans is via our kids. Listen to them; hear them. Take responsibility for your own actions without blaming your ex and see a new respect form between you and your child. They miss nothing. They know everything, and they are smarter than we often give them credit for. To all the parents out there doing their very best, well done!

Kids are amazing. Let's raise happy ones.

TOP TIPS FOR KIDS AND TEENS

- The single most important thing that you must remember is that YOU are valuable, important, beautiful and special and there is no one else quite like you on the planet.

- What you have to say matters, it always has it always will.

- Keeping your sad feelings inside you will hurt you so find someone you can share them with so you can let them out.

- You are allowed to tell other kids, teens and adults how you feel about your life and the people that directly influence it.

- If your parents divorce that is never ever your fault. Parents don't get divorced due to something their child did.

- Parents fall out of love sometimes but they don't just stop loving you, parents are not made that way.

- Parents and family members may lie to protect you or keep your mom or dad away from you. If you can't talk to them find an adult you trust that you can talk to.

- You can ask your parents not to speak badly about each other to you and you can ask your parents to make an effort to get along if that is what you need.

- It is not nor ever will be your job to please both parents, this is impossible when they divorce so do your best but do not feel guilty.

- Try to remember that your parents probably tried very hard not to divorce and it was very hard for them to break up.

- Almost all parents that divorce stay divorced. They know what is best for them.

- You may get two birthdays two Christmas's, two bedrooms and lots of other great experiences, so always look at the bright side.

- Not everyone gets divorced but if they do everyone deserves to be happy in their life.

- If your parent gets remarried, try to get along with your new step mom or dad as it can be difficult for them too.

- If you get new brothers and sisters they may have had the same experiences as you in a divorce so it's not always easy for them either.

- Do your best in all ways. Be true to yourself and always share your true feelings with your parents if you can, that way they can try to improve your home life but they are not mind readers so you will need to advise them.

- Growing up is an adventure if you choose it to be.

- Your parents were kids too once and sometimes they forget what that was like. Do your best to help them to have fun and lighten up.

- Remember, everyone on the planet has greatness and love inside of them, sometimes they just need reminding.

You can email me anytime with your stories:

Danielle@kidssoulspeak.com

www.kidssoulspeak.com

TOP TIPS FOR PARENTS

- It is possible to have a healthy friendship with your ex, it's a choice and it will serve your children's mental health and yours hugely.

- Both parents need to financially support their children in achievable ways wherever possible.

- If you earn more than your ex, be kind and respectful about them as they are more than likely doing their best.

- Be open to allowing your kids to take their best toys, clothes and gadgets with them on a visit with their other parent. Have a plan in place that serves everyone.

- Try to be nice in all communications with your ex, in time it will come back to you and you will feel better inside.

- Don't force your kids to split in two on their birthday and Christmas. You can give them a birthday on another day. You can have two Christmas days. You can switch each year with your ex on your kid's birthday. Don't put that pressure on them.

- Your role is not to please friends or family members.

- Don't blame everything you can't do with your kids on your ex.

- Please remember that your choices will influence the rest of your children's lives, so make good ones that help them.

- No kid can handle you or anyone else speaking badly about their mom or dad. Try not to bring your own personal feelings if they are negative towards their parent. This is proven to have long term emotional damage, so choose not to do this.

- If you saw good in your ex but no one else in your family did, don't forget to always share the good parts to your kids about their mom or dad. Family members and friends will never truly know why you fell in love with your children's mom or dad so don't destroy anything good that is left to say about them. Your children will always remember what you say.

- Give access to your kids and allow them to form their own relationship with the other parent as long as their lives are not in danger. Some parents deliberately use their kids as weapons and this is emotionally destructive to children. You are not helping your kids develop if you engage in this behaviour.

- Double check in with yourself to make sure you are not being overly dramatic when it comes to your memories and conversations in your 'head' about your marriage and divorce.

- Always try to play fair but do establish guidelines so you, your ex and your kids know what the plan going forward is for sharing time.

- Please don't purposely block your kids from their loving grandparents and cousins, there are laws around this now and most grandparents will do anything to keep their grandchildren safe and loved.

- Your kids are tougher than you think so don't feel guilty all your life if your marriage doesn't work out. Everyone deserves to be happy and that includes you.

- All kids dream of their parents getting back together, this is normal.

- If your kid wants a photo of their parent in their room allow it and let it go. In a short space of time you wont even notice the photo in their room and more importantly it will give your kids peace of mind and security in their heart. It is not their job to hide their other parent just because you don't like them.

- No matter what you think all kids are hard wired to love both parents, just think about how you feel about your parents. So, don't expect them to not want to contact them or to make them proud.

- I am divorced and I have had to learn ALL the above. You can do this, it takes time but everyone benefits in the long term.

- You are a good parent and your ex believes they are too. Most parents deeply love their kids they just have different ways of showing it.

- Keep your word if you plan to see your kids. Don't blame the other parent for everything. The children you are raising need both of you.

- Do your best and love yourself through raising your children, happy mom's and dad's guarantees happier kids.

TO ALL THE KIDS WHO READ THIS BOOK

I hope that you enjoyed the stories and that many of you will relate them to your own personal experiences. Always believe that you are worthy, valuable and can do anything you put your mind to. You matter. What you say, think and feel matters. I offer Kids Soul Speak to you as a platform for your voice to be heard. If this book has helped you in your own life, I would really like to hear from you if you are nineteen years of age and under. If you would like me to come and speak at your school I can share my 'kids hang out' seminar with you and your peers, it's super fun and you will leave feeling like a super hero. And if you want to email me your own story you can do it here:

Danielle@kidssoulspeak.com

www.Kidssoulspeak.com

You need permission from a parent and you need to choose a different name for yourself, so make one up that makes you feel great and don't forget to tell me your true age. Look out for my upcoming books in the Kids Soul Speak series. Email me for the questions in these books, and I may be able to include you!

The African American Kid

Kids Who See Angels, Magic and Other Amazing Things!

The Military Kid

Kids of Religion

Kids of Divorce (Part Two)

How Kids View the World

The Muslim Kid

Kids with Special Gifts

How Kids View School

To all the children and teenagers in this book: Thank you, thank you, thank you. You are brave, special, beautiful, valuable and smart. This gift we have created to help other kids and parent's is fantastic and you will help heal many that read it. You rock, I love you.

Original Art Work by LON – www.lon-art.com

Book Cover and Design by LON